Sourcebook of Contemporary Fashion Design

Marta R. Hidalgo

HARPER
DESIGN

An Imprint of HarperCollins Publishers

Sourcebook of Contemporary Fashion Design

First Edition:
Published by **maomao** publications in 2011
Via Laietana, 32 4th fl. of. 104
08003 Barcelona, España
Tel. : +34 93 268 80 88
Fax : +34 93 317 42 08
www.maomaopublications.com

English language edition first published in 2011 by:
Harper Design
An Imprint of HarperCollins*Publishers*,
10 East 53rd Street
New York, NY 10022
Tel.: (212) 207-7000
Fax: (212) 207-7654
harperdesign@harpercollins.com
www.harpercollins.com

Distributed throughout the world by:
HarperCollinsPublishers
10 East 53rd Street
New York, NY 10022
Fax: (212) 207-7654

Publisher: Paco Asensio

Editor & Texts: Marta R. Hidalgo (le mot project*)

Translation: Cillero & de Motta

Art Direction: Emma Termes Parera

Layout: Maira Purman

Cover Design: Emma Termes Parera

Library of Congress Control Number: 2011931494

Printed in China

ISBN: 978-0-06211362-7

Second Printing, 2012

Sourcebook of Contemporary Fashion Design

A&V Aganovich Ailanto Akris Albino Alma Aguilar Anna Molinari Antiatoms Antoni & Alison Antonio Miró Atsuro Tayama Avsh Alom Gur Bambi by Laura Barbara Bui Basso & Brooke Bernard Chandran Betsey Johnson Bora Aksu Carmen March Catherine Malandrino Cecilia Sörensen Claudia Rosa Lukas Comentrigo Corinne Cobson Costume National Daniel Herman Disaya Duckie Brown Edward Sexton Fabrics Interseason Fátima Lopes Francesco Smalto Gilles Rosier Gori de Palma Guy Laroche Hamish Morrow John Galliano José Miró Josep Font Juan Antonio López Juun.J Kiminori Morishita Kina Fernández Krizia Robustella La Casita de Wendy Laura B Collection Particulière Lorena Rodríguez Louis Féraud Mammifères de Luxe Martin Lamothe Masatomo Modernist Neil Barrett Phi Postweiler Hauber Rui Leonardes Sharon Wauchob Sinpatron Steve J & Yoni P Temperley London Tillmann Lauterbach Tsumori Chisato Txell Miras Victorio & Lucchino Vincenzo De Cotiis Yigal Azrouël A&V Aganovich Ailanto Akris Albino Alma Aguilar Anna Molinari Antiatoms Antoni & Alison Antonio Miró Atsuro Tayama Avsh Alom Gur Bambi by Laura Barbara Bui Basso & Brooke Bernard Chandran Betsey Johnson Bora Aksu Carmen March Catherine Malandrino Cecilia Sörensen Claudia Rosa Lukas Comentrigo Corinne Cobson Costume National Daniel Herman Disaya Duckie Brown Edward Sexton Fabrics Interseason Fátima Lopes Francesco Smalto Gilles Rosier Gori de Palma Guy Laroche Hamish Morrow John Galliano José Miró Josep Font Juan Antonio López Juun.J Kiminori Morishita Kina Fernández Krizia Robustella La Casita de Wendy Laura B Collection Particulière Lorena Rodríguez Louis Féraud Mammifères de Luxe Martin Lamothe Masatomo Modernist Neil Barrett Phi Postweiler Hauber Rui Leonardes Sharon Wauchob Sinpatron Steve J & Yoni P Temperley London Tillmann Lauterbach Tsumori Chisato Txell Miras Victorio & Lucchino Vincenzo De Cotiis Yigal Azrouël A&V Aganovich Ailanto Akris Albino Alma Aguilar Anna Molinari Antiatoms Antoni & Alison Antonio Miró Atsuro Tayama Avsh Alom Gur Bambi by Laura Barbara Bui Basso & Brooke Bernard Chandran Betsey Johnson Bora Aksu Carmen March Catherine Malandrino Cecilia Sörensen Claudia Rosa Lukas Comentrigo Corinne Cobson Costume National Daniel Herman Disaya Duckie Brown Edward Sexton Fabrics Interseason Fátima Lopes Francesco Smalto Gilles Rosier Gori de Palma Guy Laroche Hamish Morrow John Galliano José Miró Josep Font Juan Antonio López Juun.J Kiminori Morishita Kina Fernández Krizia Robustella La Casita de Wendy Laura B Collection Particulière Lorena Rodríguez Louis Féraud Mammifères de Luxe Martin Lamothe Masatomo Modernist Neil Barrett Phi Postweiler Hauber Rui Leonardes Sharon Wauchob Sinpatron Steve J & Yoni P Temperley London Tillmann Lauterbach Tsumori Chisato Txell Miras Victorio & Lucchino Vincenzo De Cotiis Yigal Azrouël A&V Aganovich Ailanto Akris Albino Alma Aguilar Anna Molinari Antiatoms Antoni & Alison Antonio Miró Atsuro Tayama Avsh Alom Gur Bambi by Laura Barbara Bui Basso & Brooke Bernard Chandran Betsey Johnson Bora Aksu Carmen March Catherine Malandrino Cecilia Sörensen Claudia Rosa Lukas Comentrigo Corinne Cobson Costume National Daniel Herman Disaya Duckie Brown Edward Sexton Fabrics Interseason Fátima Lopes Francesco Smalto Gilles Rosier Gori de Palma Guy Laroche Hamish Morrow John Galliano José Miró Josep Font Juan Antonio López Juun.J Kiminori Morishita Kina Fernández Krizia Robustella La Casita de Wendy Laura B Collection Particulière Lorena Rodríguez Louis Féraud Mammifères de Luxe Martin Lamothe Masatomo Modernist Neil Barrett Phi Postweiler Hauber Rui Leonardes Sharon Wauchob Sinpatron Steve J & Yoni P Temperley London Tillmann Lauterbach Tsumori Chisato Txell Miras Victorio & Lucchino Vincenzo De Cotiis Yigal Azrouël A&V Aganovich Ailanto Akris Albino Alma Aguilar Anna Molinari Antiatoms Antoni

08	A&V	226	Gori de Palma
16	Aganovich	230	Guy Laroche
22	Ailanto	234	Hamish Morrow
30	Akris	244	John Galliano
38	Albino	254	José Miró
44	Alma Aguilar	260	Josep Font
50	Anna Molinari	264	Juan Antonio López
56	Antiatoms	270	Juun.J
62	Antoni & Alison	276	Kiminori Morishita
68	Antonio Miró	286	Kina Fernández
74	Atsuro Tayama	292	Krizia Robustella
84	Avsh Alom Gur	298	La Casita de Wendy
90	Bambi by Laura	306	Laura B Collection Particulière
98	Barbara Bui	310	Lorena Rodríguez
108	Basso & Brooke	316	Louis Féraud
114	Bernard Chandran	324	Mammifères de Luxe
120	Betsey Johnson	330	Martin Lamothe
128	Bora Aksu	338	Masatomo
134	Carmen March	348	Modernist
142	Catherine Malandrino	354	Neil Barrett
146	Cecilia Sörensen	360	Phi
154	Claudia Rosa Lukas	366	Postweiler Hauber
160	Comentrigo	372	Rui Leonardes
166	Corinne Cobson	378	Sharon Wauchob
174	Costume National	386	Sinpatron
180	Daniel Herman	392	Steve J & Yoni P
188	Disaya	400	Temperley London
194	Duckie Brown	410	Tillmann Lauterbach
200	Edward Sexton	416	Tsumori Chisato
204	Fabrics Interseason	422	Txell Miras
210	Fátima Lopes	432	Victorio & Lucchino
216	Francesco Smalto	440	Vincenzo De Cotiis
222	Gilles Rosier	446	Yigal Azrouël

SUPERCASHMERE
Nm 2/52 - 2/80 - 3/52 - 3/80
100% Cashmere Pettinato
100% Worsted Cashmere

Fashion is constantly redefined. Throughout history, fashion has served as an eye-capturing view of the political, social, cultural, and economic climates, and what was to come, at least for the next two seasons. Although some think otherwise, clothing is not a mere adornment for the wearer, but a representation of the person who wears or chooses the garments. Fashion is a means of visibly portraying an individual's personality, sense of humor, dreams, hopes, anxieties and frustrations. In times when the body was frowned upon and was considered something embarrassing and shameful, clothes were used to hide and suppress it. When the body was viewed as "honorable" and considered something to be celebrated, fashion became a means of beautification, a form of freedom and self-expression.

Since the start of the twenty-first century, the number of design schools and students with the intention of joining the industry has grown exponentially. TV shows feature aspiring designers competing against one another. Manufacturing companies rely on material suppliers in countries where production costs are lower. Fashion consumers are more and better informed than ever before. They want to know not only who designs their favorite clothes, but also where the material for the clothes comes from—what type of animals they are wearing and in what conditions they have been reared—hence the growing interest of companies and industries to take actions that show social and environmental awareness. Withstanding these changes, a key aspect of the framework of the fashion business remains intact: the creative genius of a select few privileged aesthetes who have been, are, and will be able to materialize exactly what identifies the next step in history in the form of clothing.

Today, next generation talents are cultivated in the Paris, Milan, London and New York fashion scenes, each designer hoping to be "the next big thing" in the world of fashion. Some evoke the dreamlike and the whimsical in their lines. Some appreciate minimalist fashion. Others offer a baroque feeling of generosity to satisfy even the most luxurious, glamorous, and feminine appetites. Much of twenty-first century fashion pays tribute to past eras. Some looks evoke memories of Victorian or Gothic styles, and others evoke styles on the other end of the spectrum—such as those from the sixties, seventies, or eighties. There are also designers who can't resist the magic of contemporary art when creating their collections. They use unique highly sought-after pieces of material to understand art and visually express this understanding in their collections. What is referred to as "conceptual couture" has emerged from the interplay of modern and artistic ideas between Eastern and Western designers. The contribution of new technology into the field of fashion design has encouraged the use of materials such as nylon, microfibers, and other unusual materials such as cellulose and plastic.

It is difficult to forget about fashion. It is everywhere and soaks everything around us. Although the main concerns that drive society today seem vastly different from those twenty years ago, designers feel—with a kind of sixth sense—what, at first glance, may seem like a bleak future for their profession: the fact that the price of their designs is the only axis around which all their efforts revolve. Maybe it is true that the increasing availability of low-cost labels could mar the desire to wear the real McCoy, but the message that all respectable designers and fashion houses agree on is the importance of issues such as the working conditions in the clothing industry and the need for socially and environmentally responsible production. They all face the same challenge: how to merge high quality design ideas with responsible clothing production and market it at a price that allows them to succeed.

Our objective is to showcase the finest work of a select group of responsible fashion designers to demonstrate through their designs how they keep an eye on our ever-changing society. We created a list of today's most notable designers and labels. We then went to each one and asked them to share an inspiration, a garment, and a dream. Some designers gave multiple responses; others shared only the first response that came to them. Some spoke to the point; others lets their words and thoughts trail off. All answers, lengthy or brief, provide insight into the world of these designers and their creative minds. The designers and labels we share with you here are all of this century. They dictate trends and advocate the use of the human form as an expression of our individuality. We have highlighted the inspiration and sentiments behind individual designs and garments, as well as the moods they intended to capture. We've also provided an assortment of sketches, images, and photos to show you the looks the designers dreamed up, as well as their visual inspirations and finished products. We can choose not to follow fashion, but it is impossible to escape our own personalities, desires, and longings, which good design give us the tools to show off.

Spring-summer 2007 campaign

A&V

www.lithill.lt/a&v/

One inspiration

"Traveling in time, even if it is five minutes to the future, although two hundred years to the past would be more interesting."

In 1993, two young independent Lithuanian designers, Alex Pogrebnojus and Vida Simanaviciute, decided to work together on a new label, A&V. Simanaviciute studied design at the Kaunas Art School, while Pogrebnojus studied at the Vilnius Conservatoire in the Lithuanian capital, the city the two designers would choose for their company's offices.

A&V produces two collections each year, coinciding with the change in season: spring-summer and fall-winter. Their collections are based on a balanced mix of tradition and contemporary style. They tend to make restrained use of color, which always infuses perfectly structured, symmetrical pieces. One of their most highly regarded specialities is tailoring, where pieces are made to fit the body as part of a totally exclusive service.

The work of these designers is a feature of many plays, musicals, and performances. Paris and Vilnius are the venues where the pair hold runway shows to present their designs for the new seasons. They are also frequently showcased by magazines such as *Vogue*, *L'Officiel*, *Icon*, *W*, *Zoo* and *Fashion Daily*.

Sketches from the Homme collection fall-winter 2008-2009

One garment

"We can not distinguish one. It is the entirety that is important."

Sketches from the fall-winter 2007-2008 collection

Suit from the fall-winter 2007-2008 collection. Photo by Monika Pozerskite

"Dreams and daydreams are a secret. If you name them, the magic disappears and they may never come true…"

From left to right: Homme fall-winter 2008-2009, spring-summer 2007, spring-summer 2007 collections

Picture from the fall-winter 2008-2009 collection. Photos by Monika Pozerskite

Sketches from the fall-winter 2008-2009 (left) and fall-winter 2007-2008 collections (right)

Picture from the fall-winter 2008-2009 collection. Photos by Monika Pozerskite

Picture of the fall-winter 2008-2009 Aganovich campaign

Aganovich

www.aganovich.com

One inspiration

"To be as iconic as we are iconoclastic. To bring humor where it is least appropriate."

After meeting on St. Valentine's Day 2002, Nana Aganovich and Brooke Taylor decided to create a project that accommodated their passions. And from this wish, Aganovich, a luxury, feminine fashion label was born in 2005.

After graduating from Dansk Designskol, Nana earned a masters degree in Central Saint Martins and cofounded the Missing Sock Studio in Hong Kong. Brooke graduated in Philosophy and became a writer and collaborator for many literary and international fashion magazines such as *Purple Magazine*, *Dune*, *Ryuko Tsushin*, *Big Magazine* and *Colors*. In 2005, they launched the Aganovich project, which they presented at London Fashion Week.

Nana is the head of design for Aganovich and Brooke proposes the theme and the conceptual influences of each collection. The Aganovich label is based on the fusion of strict feminine lines with materializing conceptual lines that respond to expression founded on the art of seduction. Nana and Brooke design simple pieces with well-defined volumes. They have a clear preference for neutral colors.

With the experience of a few collections behind them, Aganovich has the fashion press from around the world on their side and they have taken part in side projects such as a documentary that deals with the business policies of the world of fashion for Nick Knight's SHOWstudio.

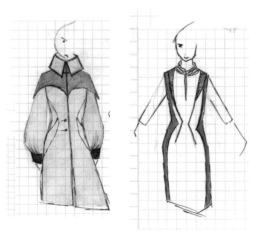

Sketches from the fall-winter 2008-2009 collection

One garment

"A coat that you can wear with nothing underneath."

Pictures from the fall-winter 2008-2009 collection runway show

Picture from the fall-winter 2008-2009 collection runway show

Sketches from the fall-winter 2008-2009 collection

One dream

"To buy a donkey."

 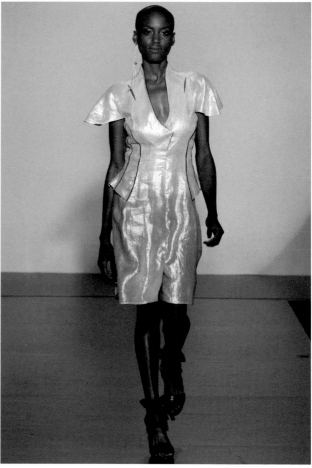

Pictures from the fall-winter 2008-2009 collection runway show

Sketches from the fall-winter 2006-2007 collection

Ailanto

www.ailanto.com

One inspiration

"Faye Dunaway's look in the film *Eyes of Laura Mars* (Columbia Pictures Corporation, 1978), the New Yorker at the end of the seventies with an insight into the disco era of the eighties."

Ailanto is a fashion label formed by twin brothers Iñaki and Aitor Muñoz, born in Bilbao, Spain in 1968. Their headquarters is in Barcelona, where both designers graduated in fine arts from the University of Barcelona. Iñaki combined these studies with a fashion design degree from the Institude de Artes Visuais.

Ailanto's fashion is characterized by recreation of a visual universe filled with geometric forms where the combination of colors, the play on symmetry and references to avant-garde artistic movements are ever-present. Their patterns are a kaleidoscope of colors that, at times, involve unconventional color combinations. Red, brown, blue, and grass green are their favorite colors. Their designs have a linear and detailed style and they are clearly passionate about garments such as coats, dresses and skirts.

Since 1999, they have participated in the Prêt-à-Porter Paris show (Atmosphère) and in the designer's week workshops in Paris and in Tranoï. Since 2002, the Ailanto collections have been presented at the Pasarela Cibeles in Madrid. In November 2004, Ailanto received the award for Best Designer from *Glamour* magazine. In addition to their fashion designs, Ailanto also designs homeware. Their main international markets are Japan, the UK, Hong Kong, the USA, Belgium and Italy.

Final scene of the spring-summer 2008 runway show

Above: two sketches from the spring-summer 2004 (left) and spring-summer 2005 collections (right)
Below: sketches from the fall-winter 2004-2005 collection

One garment

"A tweed raincoat."

Above: sketches from fall-winter 2004-2005 (left) and spring-summer 2006 collections (right)
Below: sketches from spring-summer 2006, spring-summer 2004 and fall-winter 2004-2005 collections

Sketches from the spring-summer 2006 collection

One dream

"To open up stores in Barcelona and Madrid."

 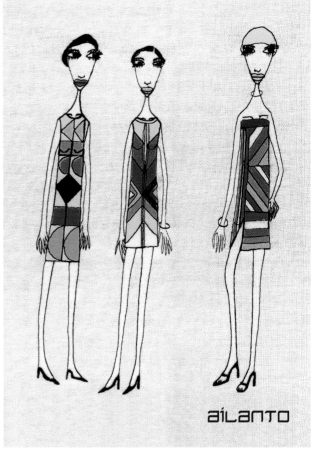

Sketches from the spring-summer 2005 and spring-summer 2006 campaigns

Pictures from the spring-summer 2008 and fall-winter 2008-2009 collections

Picture from the fall-winter 2008-2009 collection runway show

Akris

www.akris.ch

One inspiration

"Architecture."

The designer Albert Kriemler is a clear example of fusion between the classic values of a fashion designer and traditional couture. Swiss by birth, Albert's dream was to design for Saks Fifth Avenue or Bergdorf Goodman in New York. He ended up taking charge of Akris, the family business founded by his grandmother.

Akris' collections are based on a love of fabric, color and architecture, hence their references to "building" garments or the search for the best proportions along with the use of the best Italian fabrics created by textile designers from the provinces of Biella and Como. Meanwhile, they never gave up on their quest to add new touches to fabrics such as cashmere, wool, silk, cotton or linen.

Albert's work with the Akris and Akris Punto design teams in St. Gallen (Switzerland) is carried out far from the frenzy of the main fashion capitals. The designer requires a peaceful working environment where he can concentrate, with the help of a team of professionals with whom he shares the same language and a single philosophy. His most loyal customers are Susan Sarandon, Brooke Shields and Princess Caroline of Monaco. All Akris collections are manufactured in different workshops in Tesino, St. Gallen and Zurich.

Sketches from fall-winter 2005-2006 and fall-winter 2007-2008

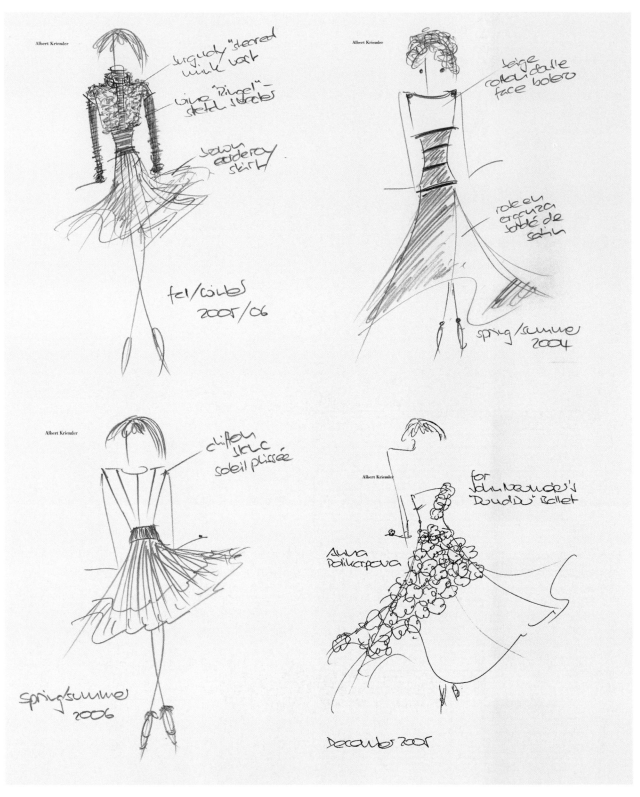

Clockwise from top right: sketches from the fall-winter 2005-2006, spring-summer 2004, spring-summer 2006 collections and the sketch for Anna Polikarpova's dress, a ballet dancer for the Hamburg Ballet (2005)

Picture from the fall-winter 2008-2009 collection runway show

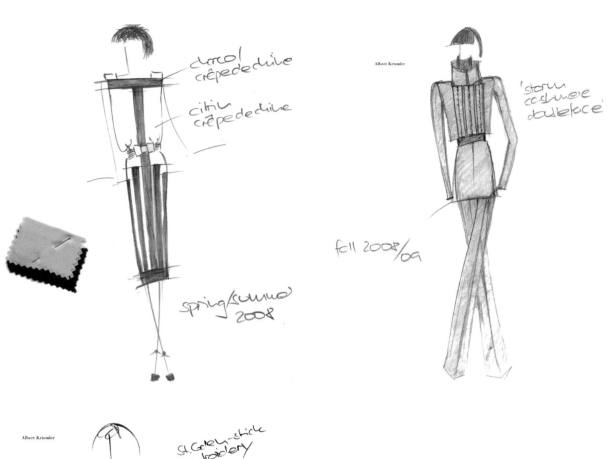

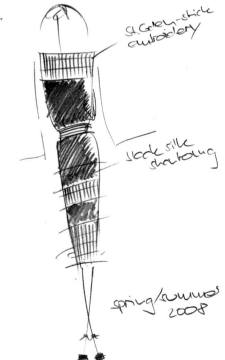

charcol
crêpe de chine

citrin
crêpe de chine

spring/summer
2008

'storm'
cashmere
doubleface'

fall 2008/09

Albert Kriemler

Albert Kriemler

St. Galler-stitch
embroidery

black silk
shantung

spring/summer
2008

One garment

"The hand-crafted steel belt in chrome, pewter, matte or lacquered black."

Sketches from the spring-summer 2008 and fall-winter 2008-2009 collections

Picture from the fall-winter 2008-2009 campaign

Pictures from the fall-winter 2008-2009 collection runway show

"To show my collection in the Garden of Tuileries by Jacques and Peter Wirtz in front of the I. M. Pei's pyramid and the Louvre part by Jacques Lemercier."

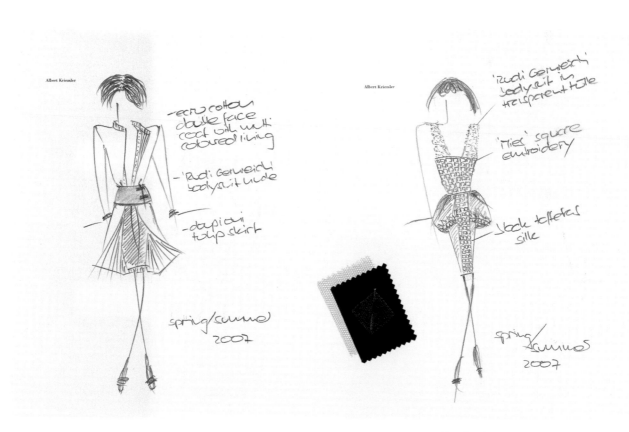

Sketches from spring-summer 2007 collections

Sketches from the summer 2006 collection

Albino

www.albino-fenizia.com

One inspiration

"The couture pieces themselves."

Born in Rome with a Neapolitan father and French-Italian mother, Albino D'Amato studied architecture in Rome and a year of industrial design in Turin, where he worked for the auto-maker Fiat. When he turned twenty, he moved to Paris, where he studied fashion design at the renowned École de la Chambre Syndicale de la Couture Parisienne, run by the French Fashion Federation. His career in fashion design has been meteoric. He has worked for some of the most prestigious in the business. He started out with Ungaro, followed by periods with Guy Laroche, Kenzo Jungle, Emilio Pucci and Atelier Versace.

When Albino returned to Italy, he worked with the Dolce & Gabbana design team in Milan until he was offered a position with Giorgio Armani, the firm he worked for until he opened his own label, Albino. After several setbacks on the business side, however, with the help of his current partner, Gianfranco Fenizia, he presented his first collection at the 2004 Milan Fashion Week.

Albino's designs are for a very feminine, urban woman and feature perfectly defined silhouettes. His pieces are on sale in retail establishments such as Penelope in Brescia, Biffi in Milan, Maria Luisa in Paris, Shine and Harvey Nichols in Hong Kong, Princess in Antwerp, Midwest in Tokyo, Lide in Moscow, and Belinda in Sydney.

Sketches of the looks presented at the Albino show in Milan (2006)

One garment

"Dresses in general."

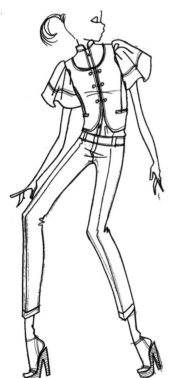

Sketch from the summer 2006 collection

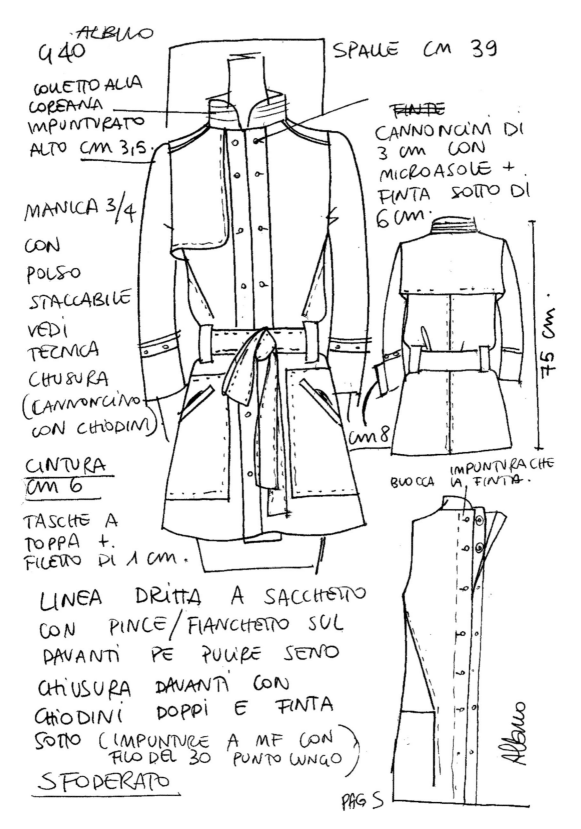

ALBINO

G 40

SPALLE CM 39

COLLETTO ALLA COREANA IMPUNTURATO ALTO CM 3,5.

~~FINTE~~ CANNONCINI DI 3 CM CON MICROASOLE + FINTA SOTTO DI 6 CM.

MANICA 3/4 CON POLSO STACCABILE VEDI TECNICA CHIUSURA (CANNONCINO CON CHIODINI)

CINTURA CM 6

TASCHE A TOPPA + FILETTO DI 1 CM.

LINEA DRITTA A SACCHETTO CON PINCE/FIANCHETTO SUL DAVANTI PE PULIRE SENO

CHIUSURA DAVANTI CON CHIODINI DOPPI E FINTA SOTTO (IMPUNTURE A MF CON FILO DEL 30 PUNTO LUNGO)

SFODERATO

CM 8

75 CM

BLOCCA IMPUNTURA CHE LA FINTA.

Albino

PAG 5

Sketch from the summer 2006 collection

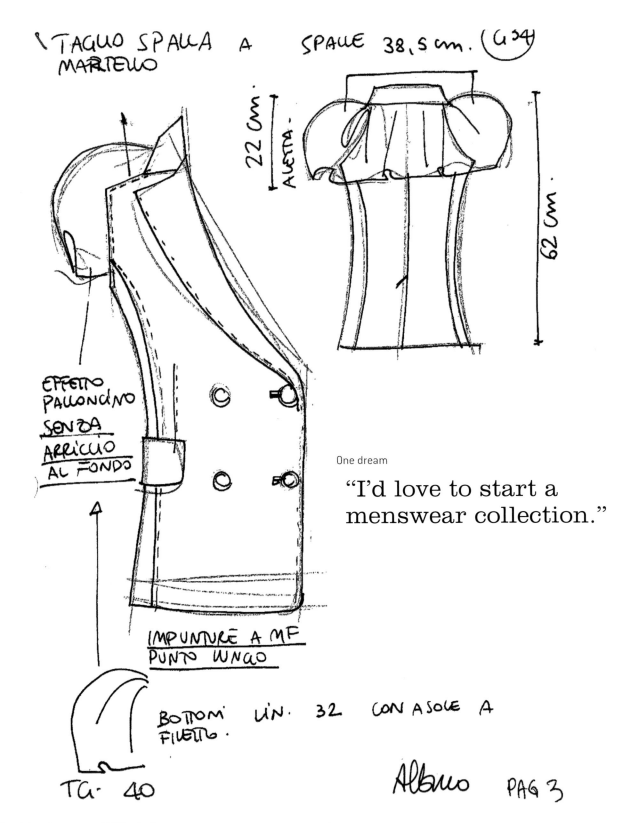

TAGLIO SPALLA A   SPALLE 38,5 cm. (G34)
MARTELLO

22 cm   ALETTA.

62 cm

SPALLE 38,5 cm. (G34)

EFFETTO
PALLONCINO
SENZA
ARRICCIO
AL FONDO

IMPUNTURE A MF
PUNTO UNICO

One dream

"I'd love to start a
menswear collection."

TG. 40

BOTTONI LIN. 32   CON ASOLE A
FILETTO.

Albino   PAG 3

Sketch from the summer 2006 collection

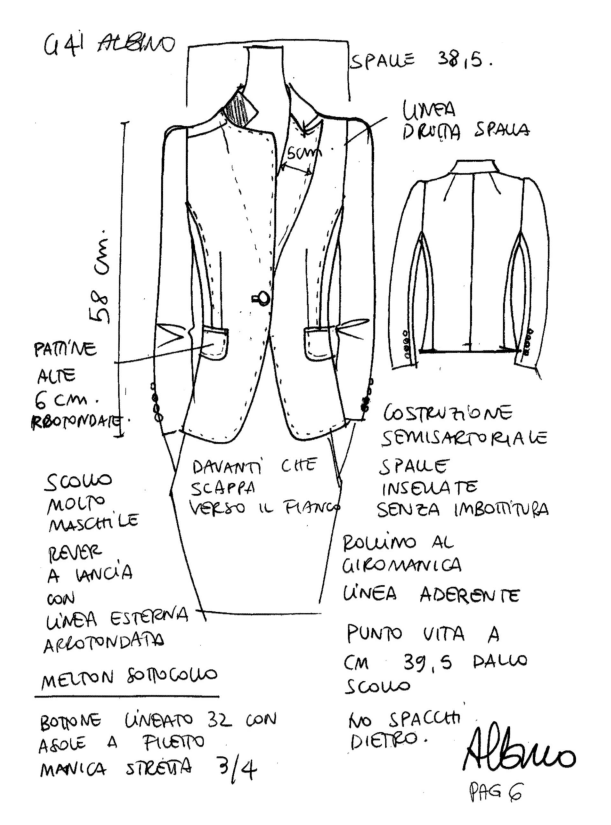

G 41 ALBINO

SPALLE 38,5.

LINEA DRITTA SPALLA

5cm

58 cm.

PATTINE ALTE 6 CM. RIBOTONDATE.

DAVANTI CHE SCAPPA VERSO IL FIANCO

SCOLLO MOLTO MASCHILE

REVER A LANCIA CON LINEA ESTERNA ARROTONDATA

MELTON SOTTOCOLLO

BOTTONE LINEATO 32 CON ASOLE A FILETTO
MANICA STRETTA 3/4

COSTRUZIONE SEMISARTORIALE

SPALLE INSELLATE SENZA IMBOTTITURA

ROLLINO AL GIROMANICA

LINEA ADERENTE

PUNTO VITA A CM 39,5 DALLO SCOLLO

NO SPACCHI DIETRO.

Albino

PAG 6

Sketch from the summer 2006 collection

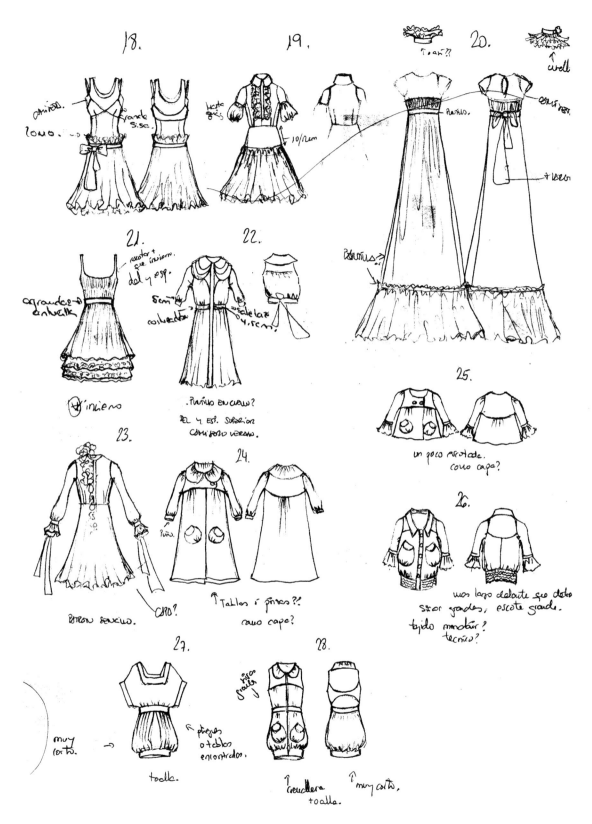

Sketches from the spring-summer 2008 collection

Alma Aguilar

www.almaaguilar.com

One inspiration

"Everything in general and nothing in particular."

Born in Madrid, Alma Aguilar's sensitivity for anything creative was awoken by her family's connection to the art world—her father is a jazz musician and her mother is a painter and poet. She studied fashion design, illustration and patternmaking at the Escuela Superior de Técnicas Industriales de la Confección de Madrid, an industrial dressmaking school. She supplemented her studies with her innate passion for drawing.

Alma set up her own label in 1998 and opened her first store a year later—it would become her showroom and subsequently her wedding dress atelier. Her style is an intelligent mix of comfort and formal. Day and night wear is brought together in creative pieces that can be worn at any hour. She took part in the Cibeles Madrid Fashion Week for the first time in 2001 and was chosen to participate in the Fashion Program organized in collaboration with the Spanish Foreign Trade Institute (ICEX) in 2003 to promote Spanish fashion in London through the Yellow Door Agency. Her designs have appeared in the UK editions of *Vogue*, *Elle*, and *Marie Claire*, and in the *How To Spend It* supplement of the *Financial Times*.

Alma has showrooms in Spain and New York, and her designs are on sale in the USA, Australia, Japan, China, Italy, Spain, and the UK in establishments such as Harvey Nichols, Tsum, Dover St Market, and Bergdorf Goodman.

Sketches from the spring-summer 2008 collection

Sketches from the spring-summer 2007 collection

Sketch from the spring-summer 2007 collection

One garment

"The layered look."

Pictures from the fall-winter 2008-2009 collection runway show

Pictures from the fall-winter 2008-2009 collection runway show

Blumarine®

Sketch from the fall-winter 2007-2008 collection

Anna
Molinari

www.blumarine.com

One inspiration

"The flowers of my garden."

The vivacious Anna Molinari is one of the most iconic designers in the history of Italian fashion. In 1977, she and her husband Gianpaolo Tarabini created Blumarine, a name inspired by their love for the blue of the sea. It was immediately awarded The Best, a prize bestowed by an international jury during a ceremony held at the Petit Palais in Paris.

Several years later she created a prêt-à-porter line for young women called Blugirl, which represents what she identifies with—youth and the joy of life. Her love of traveling, music, and painting are always present, in both her life and her collections. Some of her pieces, such as the t-shirt printed with roses, her favorite flower, have become trendy. Fashion design for Anna is the result of mixing sensations and cultural influences, and her pieces are always designed with a sensual, feminine, and dynamic woman in mind—a modern woman, like herself.

Blumarine advertising campaigns have been immortalized by such inspirational photographers as Helmut Newton and Albert Watson, and have featured the faces of leading models including Eva Herzigova, Cindy Crawford, Helena Christensen, Carla Bruni, Carré Otis, and Monica Bellucci. Anna was given a special award for her career in 2004 by the National Chamber of Italian Fashion at an event held at Milan's Royal Palace.

Sketches from the fall-winter 2007-2008 collection

Sketches from the fall-winter 2007-2008 collection

One garment

"A silk embroidered dress."

Sketch from the fall-winter 2007-2008 collection

Sketches from the fall-winter 2007-2008 collection

One dream

"To keep designing romantic and sensual dresses which can make any woman's dream come true."

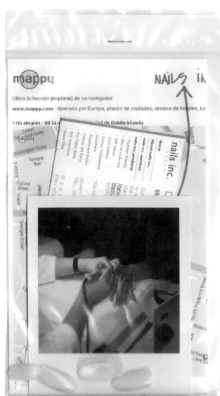

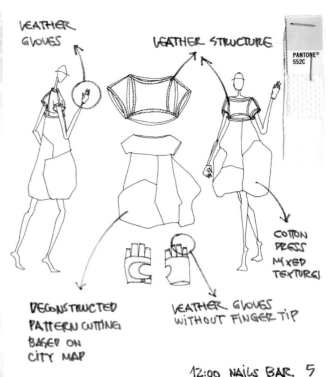

LEATHER GLOVES

LEATHER STRUCTURE

PANTONE 552C

COTTON DRESS MIXED TEXTURES

DECONSTRUCTED PATTERN CUTTING BASED ON CITY MAP

LEATHER GLOVES WITHOUT FINGER TIP

12:00 NAILS BAR. 5

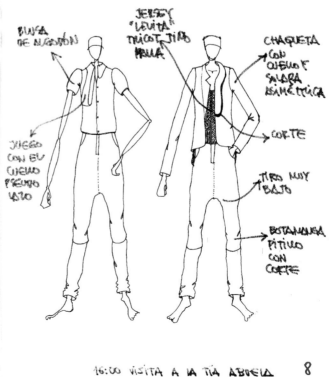

BLUSA DE ALGODÓN

JERSEY "LEVITA" TRICOT TIRO MALLA

CHAQUETA CON CUELLO E SOLAPA ASIMÉTRICA

JUEGO CON EL CUELLO PSEUDO USO

CORTE

TIRO MUY BAJO

BOTAMANGA PITILLO CON CORTE

16:00 VISITA A LA TÍA ABUELA   8

Sketches from the Picnolepsia spring-summer 2008 collection

Antiatoms

www.antiatoms.com

One inspiration

"A library."

The trio Antiatoms, formed by Aránzazu Moreno, Alejandra Salvatore and Sofía Uquillas, was born as a multi-disciplinary project in 2005 when the three studied together in the Istituto Europeo di Design. In spite of the fact that each of them comes from a different discipline (architecture, plastic arts and museography, and art direction), they have managed to complement each other's specialities and individual aesthetics. The result is a creative laboratory in which a moderate use of color, experimentation and transformation are the core themes.

Their first collection, Picnolepsia, inspired by lapses of consciousness and the recreation of a fictitious city, results in an entirely urban collection with garments suitable to be worn twenty-four hours a day. They surprised with their next collection Mik_val_exe, with white being the only color used, and with 0+1=a, the title of their latest collection, comprising garments designed on the premises of the Dadaism movement.

The Antiatoms project was based on the conceptual process of creating garments, and now extends from the development of corporate image campaigns to costume design. Their work appears on the digital headlines of *Another*, *Icon*, and *Apartment Magazine*. Recently they have customized the classic Vans trainers to sell as a limited edition style for the brand.

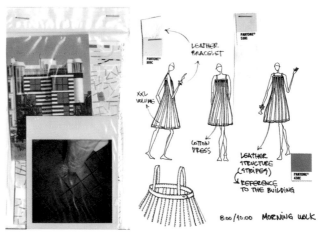

Sketches from the Picnolepsia spring-summer 2008 collection

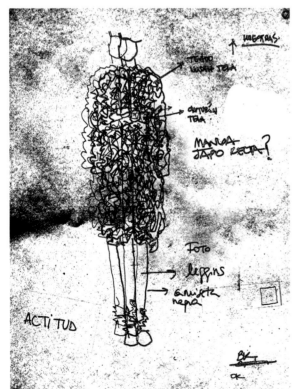

One garment

"Any of Chalayan's garment/furniture dresses."

Sketches from the 0+1=a fall-winter 2007-2008 collection. Clockwise from top left: collection logo 0+1=a, Hug coat and Attitude coat

Fig. 58 Ensamble de ... o.

Sketches from the Mik_val_exe spring-summer 2007 collection

One dream

"Eight hours
of sleep."

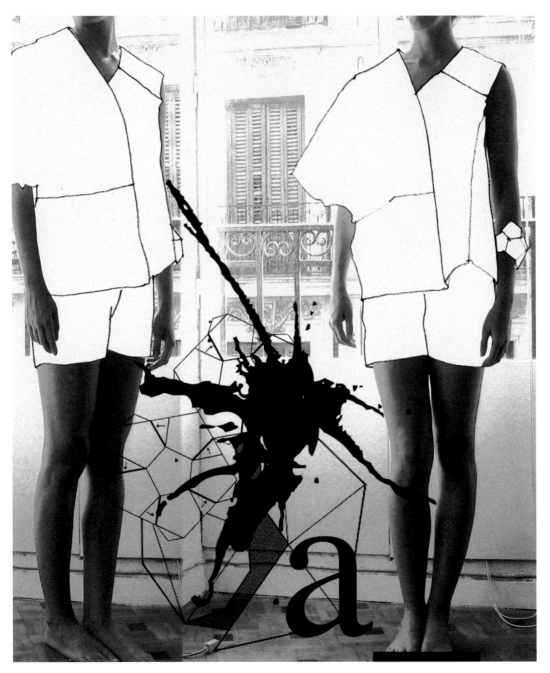

Sketches from the Mik_val_exe spring-summer 2007 collection

Sketches from the Mik_val_exe spring-summer 2007 collection

Sketch from the Be Happy spring-summer 2006 collection

Antoni
& Alison

www.antoniandalison.co.uk

"We have always been attracted to someone, a kind of naturally arty girl."

The history of Antoni and Alison started at the Central Saint Martins College of Art & Design, where Antoni studied textile and fashion design, and Alison studied fine arts and painting. Since then, they have been inseparable and when they finished their studies in 1987, they created the label Antoni & Alison. Their first collection Be Happy focused on one single garment: the t-shirt.

During their first five years working together, they designed ten complete collections. Then they reinvented their working method and decided to spend six months concentrating their efforts and creative ingenuity on redesigning the concept, the cut and the finish of their most valued garment, the t-shirt. Later, they decided to create a prêt-à-porter line that included knitwear, dresses, shirts, skirts, bags, purses and obviously the t-shirts that they are famous for. Their style is a mixture of inspirations from different decades, mainly the fifties and sixties.

In 1997, the Victoria & Albert Museum created the Antoni & Alison living file to honor the work and designs of the original couple. The museum was home to their first fashion show during the 1998 London Fashion Week. However, the room was too small and so they moved to the Royal Court Theatre, where in 2001 they organized a fashion show with a performance that had resounding success.

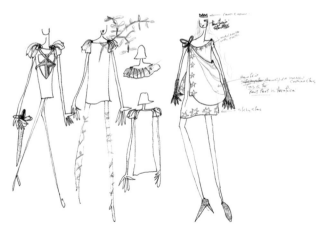

Sketch from the Be Happy spring-summer 2006 collection

HORSE 'T'.

Scenic mini skirt

Sketch from the Titanic spring-summer 2007 collection (left) and sketches from the Be Happy spring-summer 2006 collection (middle and right)

One garment

"Shoes."

Sketches of balloon dresses for spring-summer 2007

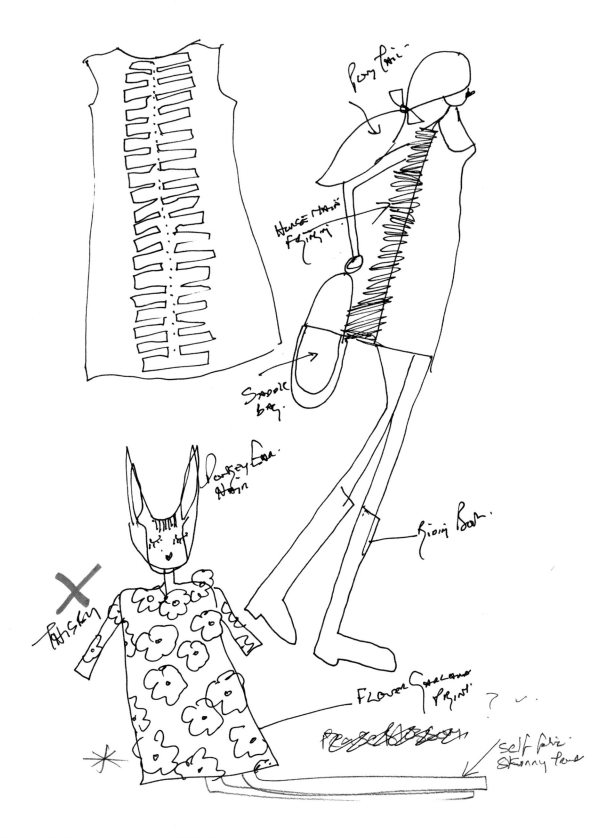

Sketch from the Be Happy spring-summer 2006 collection

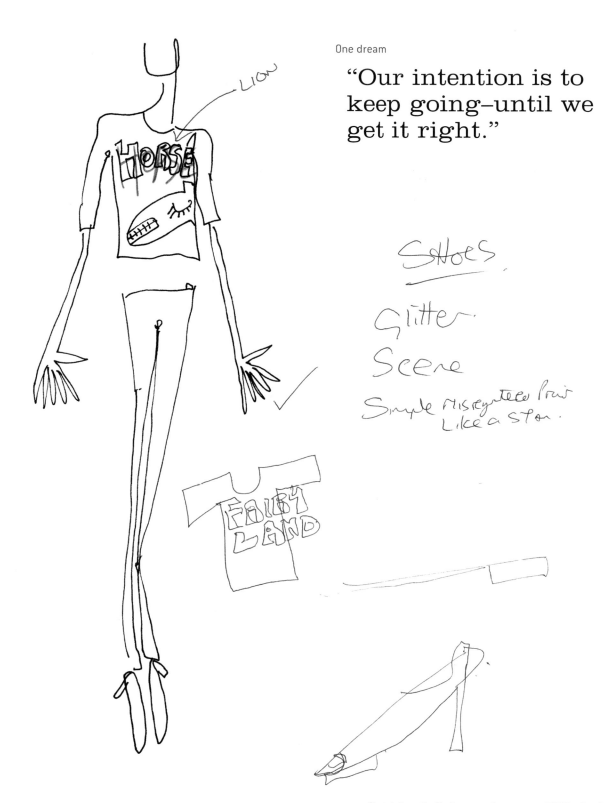

"Our intention is to keep going–until we get it right."

Sketch from the Be Happy spring-summer 2006 collection

Sketches from the fall-winter 2005-2006 collection

Antonio Miró

www.antoniomiro.es

"Zen philosophy."

Born in Barcelona in 1947, Antonio Miró studied his trade at his father's tailoring shop. This beginnings has made him into one of the most internationally-recognized Spanish designers. At the age of twenty, he opened his own store, Groc, with clothes for men and women. It was a huge success at a time when Spanish design was practically non-existent.

In 1976, he created the label Antonio Miró, which was pioneering for the local market. He gained significant renown with it as he presented his collections in Europe and the USA. He received the Cristóbal Balenciaga Award for best Spanish designer in 1988. The simplicity of his style complements the perfect construction of his pieces, made from soft and natural fabrics. His clothes have a very personal touch.

Antonio seeks originality in his shows. He was the first to put ordinary people from the street, with ages between eighteen and seventy-five, on the runway instead of models. He currently shows in Paris to give his label international projection. His has his own stores in Madrid, Osaka, Nagoya, and Tokyo. The label also has two outlet stores. He recently opened a store in Barcelona that defines the Antonio Miró universe, and where you can find clothes, floor tiles, and bedding, among other items, and he will soon be opening franchises around the world.

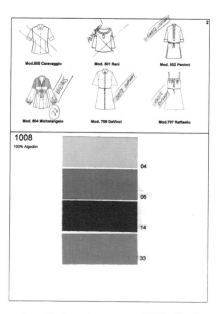

Color card used in the spring-summer 2006 collection

Sketch from the fall-winter 2005-2006 collection

Vellut ratllat
Jakytex

4.090,-
APProx

1.135 -

Jackytex
JAKYTEX
MIRA 815.

Vellut Jakytex

Ⓜ

06380

One garment

"A man's suit."

Sketch from the fall-winter 2005-2006 collection

05376

05373

PANA (FALDA

Sketch from the fall-winter 2005-2006 collection

One dream

"To never stop growing."

Sketch from the fall-winter 2005-2006 collection

2006 A/w

2006

Sketches from the fall-winter 2006-2007 collection

Atsuro Tayama

qg@quartier-general.com

One inspiration

"Underground vs. conservative."

Born in Kumamoto in 1955, Atsuro Tayama is one of Japan's most influential contemporary designers. From his very beginnings as a designer, his clothes have been known for their intellectual structure with a romantic touch. He graduated from the Bunka Fashion College in 1975, shortly after winning the prestigious Pierre Cardin Fashion Prize. Tayama would later work for Yohji Yamamoto as head of design in Europe between 1978 and 1982, and for Cacharel in the early nineties before setting up his own label, Atsuro Tayama, and developing his AT Collection line. He is also the head of brands like INDIVI, OZOC, and the Japanese label Boycott. He launched his new line, Atsuro Tayama Green Label, in 1999.

From his Paris base, Tayama has created a revolutionary style. His special way of drawing a simple outline and his way of constructing garments opened the door to a new kind of austerity that refuses to glorify forms.

Atsuro is a designer who has managed to keep a perfect balance between Oriental and Western cultures, the source of his interest in exploring shape, color, and fabrics. He projects them around the body in an original way for coexistence between Oriental tradition and Western style, as in his recent collections, where the look was strongly linked to the style of King Arthur's court.

Sketches from the fall-winter 2008-2009 collection

Above: sketches from the fall-winter 2006-2007 collection (left) and from the spring-summer 2006 collection (right)
Below: sketches from the spring-summer 2006 collection

One garment

"Men's tuxedo."

Sketch from the spring-summer 2006 collection

To
ESQUIRE

2006 S/S.

Sketch from the spring-summer 2006 collection

Sketches from the fall-winter 2008-2009 collection

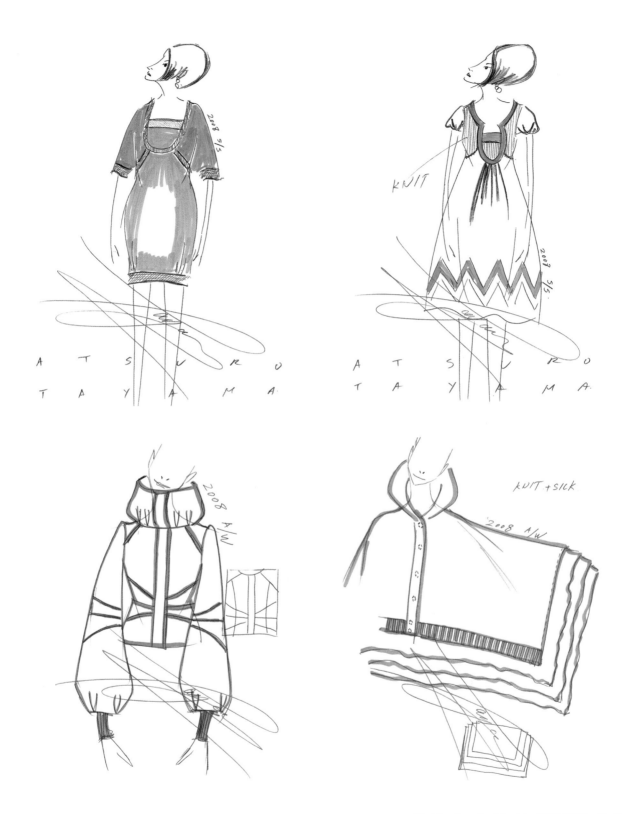

Sketches from the fall-winter 2008-2009 collection

One dream

"Continuing with my work."

Pictures from the spring-summer 2006 collection runway show

Picture from the fall-winter 2006-2007 collection runway show

Sketches from the fall-winter 2002-2003 and spring-summer 2004 collections

Avsh
Alom Gur

www.avshalomgur.com

One inspiration

"Eastern and Western elements with urban street graffiti and underground grunge. Poverty and luxury blend when designing."

London-based designer Avsh Alom Gur graduated with a distinction from Central Saint Martins College of Art & Design in 2002. He then worked for top fashion labels like Chloé, Donna Karan, Roberto Cavalli, and Nicole Farhi, where he gained the experience to create his own label. In 2005, after receiving the Topshop New Gen Award shortly thereafter, he made his debut with his first fashion show at the Museum of Natural History at London Fashion Week.

The following year, he decided to present his collection outside London Fashion Week's official program, choosing the Royal Academies of Arts as the perfect venue. Gur received rave reviews from critics following the show, especially for his baby doll dresses and pleated tops. His handmade ponchos with semi-precious stones, inspired by the apparel of the Bedouin tribes, were also praised.

In April 2005, Gur took part in the Fashion Fusion project, which brings the UK and China together, and during which the mayors of Shanghai and London signed a collaborative agreement to promote both cities. Gur was selected to represent British talent at Shanghai Fashion Week, and there he received the award for the Best Young Designer in the Shanghai International Young Fashion Designer Showcase. Today, he continues to present his collection in London at the Royal Academy of Arts.

Sketch from the spring-summer 2004 collection

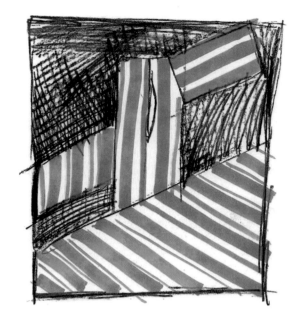

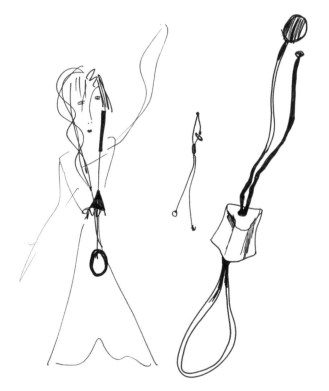

One garment

"Evening dresses, ponchos and twisted babydolls."

Sketches from the fall-winter 2006-2007 collection

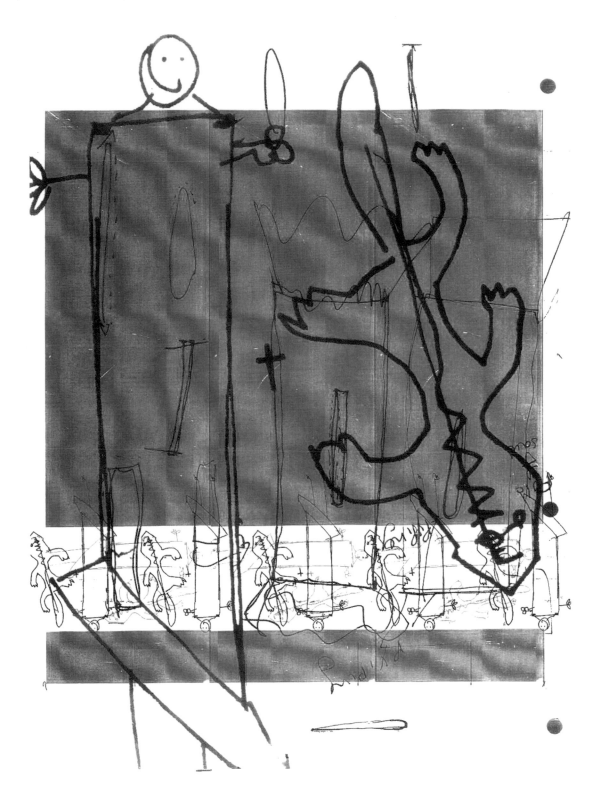

Sketch from the fall-winter 2002-2003 collection

Picture from the fall-winter 2006-2007 collection

One dream

"To not stop creating."

Pictures from the fall-winter 2006-2007 collection

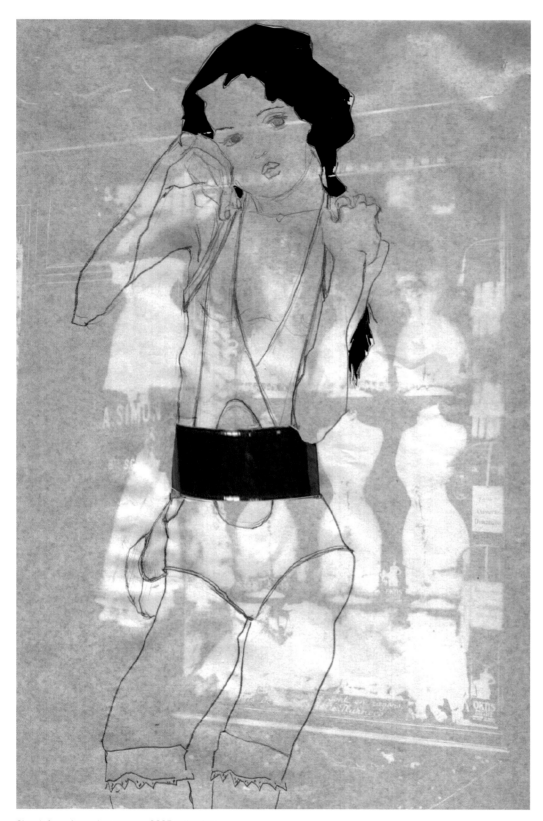

Sketch from the spring-summer 2007 collection

Bambi
by Laura

www.bambibylaura.com

One inspiration

"The imperfect searching for perfection."

Bambi by Laura is the label by a young Barcelona designer, Laura Figueras. After graduating from the Escola Superior de Disseny (ESDi) in her native city, she moved to the UK to study at the Winchester School of Art in Southampton. After finishing her studies, she worked first with Preen in London. Then in 2003, she became head of design at Women's Secret, and before the year ended she had created her own label.

Since creating Bambi by Laura at the age of twenty-three, Laura has presented six collections on catwalks such as Circuit Barcelona, Circuit Lisboa and Pasarela Barcelona. Her garments are the perfect combination of all that we conceive to be modern and harmonious. She stands out for the combination of strong colors such as pink, yellow or blue on perfectly sketched silhouettes. Her designs are complex and sophisticated.

Laura has participated in international projects such as Absolut Label 2006, designed an exclusive collection for Red Bull, and worked with the Motorola Fashion Calendar. Her garments have appeared in fashion magazines such as *i-D*, *Nylon*, *Purple*, *Spoon*, *Vogue*, and *Elle*. Bambi by Laura designs can be found on sale around the world: Olga in Paris, Pineal Eye in London, Dernier Cri in New York or Faline in Tokyo.

Photomontage with designs from the spring-summer 2007 collection

Picture from the fall-winter 2008-2009 campaign. Photos by Albert Mollón

One garment

"Vintage clothing."

Picture from the fall-winter 2008-2009 campaign. Photo by Albert Mollón

Picture from the fall-winter 2008-2009 campaign. Photos by Albert Mollón

Picture from the fall-winter 2008-2009 campaign. Photos by Albert Mollón

Picture from the fall-winter season 2008-2009. Photos by Nacho Alegre

One dream

"To continue to work and grow."

Photomontage with designs for the spring-summer 2007 collection

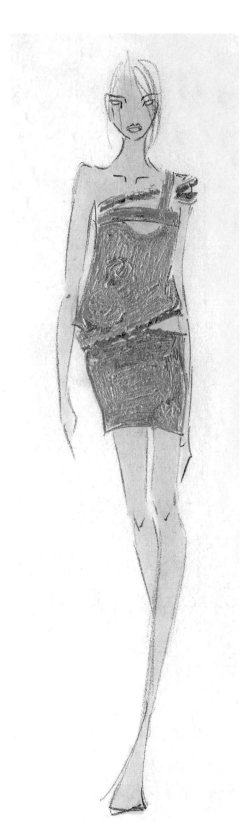

Picture and sketch from the fall-winter 2008-2009 collection

Barbara Bui

www.barbarabui.com

One inspiration

"The fresh couture."

Born in Paris to a Vietnamese father and a French mother, Barbara Bui entered the world of fashion by opening a studio-store on rue de Turbigo in Paris in 1983. Four years later, she organized her first fashion show in the French capital, and in 1998 the Initials Barbara Bui line was launched with a long line of followers as a result of the feminine and androgynous trousers included in the collection.

In 1999, Barbara Bui made her debut at New York Fashion Week at the same time as she opened her first shop in the center of Soho. One year later, she launched her first collection of luxurious accessories, which established her as a successful designer. Her pieces are a fetish for the most selective fashion editors around the planet. Her fashion shows—not-to-be-missed dates—and her campaigns have been photographed by the likes of David Bailey. Her designs typically include well-defined, perfectly cut pieces, where neutral colors are always present, and intricate garment details are perfected.

In 2003, she created a new line, Bui de Barbara Bui, a catalogue of refined casual pieces, and she was chosen unanimously to become a member of the Chambre Syndicale de la Haute Couture et des Créaterus de Mode. She has seven stores and has shows during Pret-à-Porter Paris Fashion Week.

Sketches from the fall-winter 2008-2009 collection

Runway show pictures and sketches from the fall-winter 2008-2009 collection

"A pair of sexy trousers, a chiffon top."

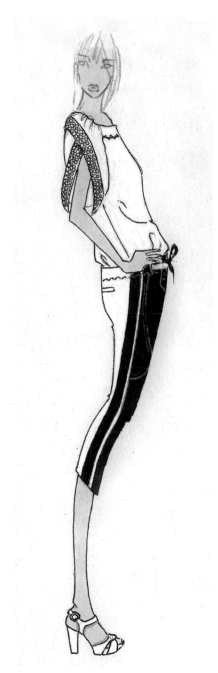

Runway show picture and sketch from the fall-winter 2008-2009 collection

Picture and sketch from the fall-winter 2008-2009 collection

Picture and sketch from the fall-winter 2008-2009 collection

Picture and sketch from the fall-winter 2008-2009 collection

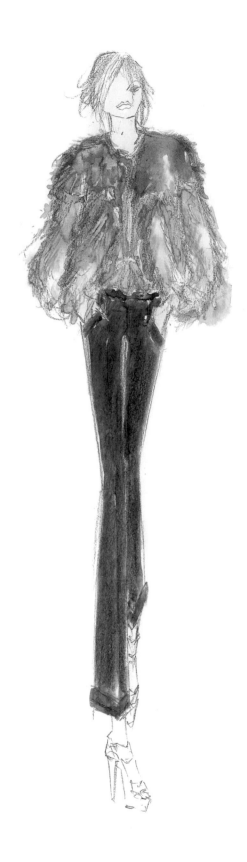

Picture and sketch from the fall-winter 2008-2009 collection

One dream

"To express the female emotional sensitivity."

Runway show sketches and pictures from the fall-winter 2008-2009 collection

Runway show pictures and sketches from the fall-winter 2008-2009 collection

Picture from the fall-winter 2007-2008 runway show

Basso & Brooke

www.bassoandbrooke.com

One inspiration

"The thin layer between reality and the imaginary."

British illustrator and graphic designer Christopher Brooke and Brazilian fashion designer Bruno Basso joined forces to create Basso & Brooke, an explosive cocktail of British style and Brazilian exoticism.

In 2004, they won a prestigious Fashion Fringe Award with an exuberant and sensual collection that was both classic and liberal, a kind of free liberated orgiastic sexual carnival with power allegories. Since then, Basso & Brooke have formed part of the group of international designers with great prospect as shown by their distribution agreement with the Aeffe Group, which also works with Alberta Ferretti, Moschino, Narciso Rodriguez, Jean Paul Gaultier and Pollini.

Their collections feature a wide range of emotion and materials: from the exuberance displayed in their 2004 collection to the use of medieval images, high tech graphics or Japanese inspiration on garments conceived according to the principles of traditional tailoring, with an abundance of color added to all of the above. Their showroom is in London; their garments are sold around all the fashion capitals in the world.

Fabric samples used in the spring-summer 2006 collection

Sketches of designs from the spring-summer 2007 collection

One garment

"Anything not boring or monotonous."

Sketches of designs from the spring-summer 2007 collection

One dream

"To develop our label in all areas."

Pictures from the fall-winter 2007-2008 collection runway show

Picture from the fall-winter 2007-2008 runway show

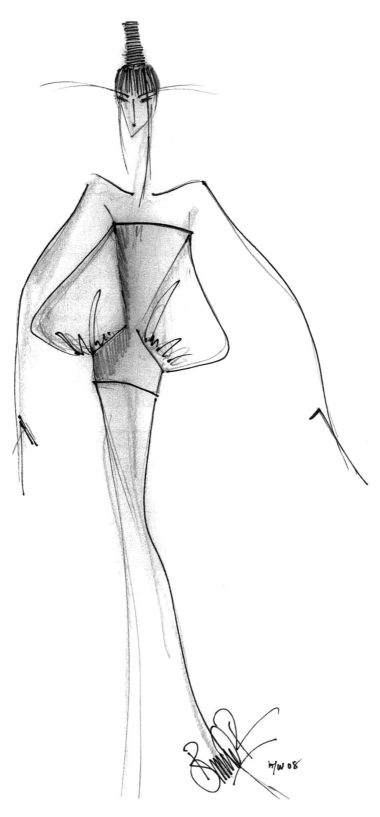

Sketch from the fall-winter 2007-2008 collection

Bernard
Chandran

www.bernardchandran.com

One inspiration

"My wife."

Raised in Kuala Lumpur, Malaysia, Bernard Chandran graduated in fine arts from the Paris American Academy and the French Fashion Federation's school École de la Chambre Syndicale de la Couture Parisienne. His talent was quickly acknowledged and he was the first non-European winner of the Silk Cut Young Designers Award and the Open European Contest for Look of the Year in 1991.

After graduating in 1993, he went home and started his own label. His collections are a retake on the standard pieces of traditional Malay dress such as *kebayas* and *kurungs*. His style features very feminine forms and silhouettes, with clean lines and exquisite and custom adorned fabrics.

Chandran opened his first European store in London's Knightsbridge district in 2004, presenting his collection at London Fashion Week the same year. His pieces are currently on sale in Europe, Dubai, and the Far East. He is still headquartered in Kuala Lumpur and has become the chief designer for artists and figures such as the royal family of Brunei. The Malaysian edition of *Tatler* chose him as one of the most outstanding Asians of the time, and he was made a Dato, an honorary title granted to him by the Sultan of Pahang for his contribution to Malaysian fashion.

Sketches from the fall-winter 2007-2008 collection

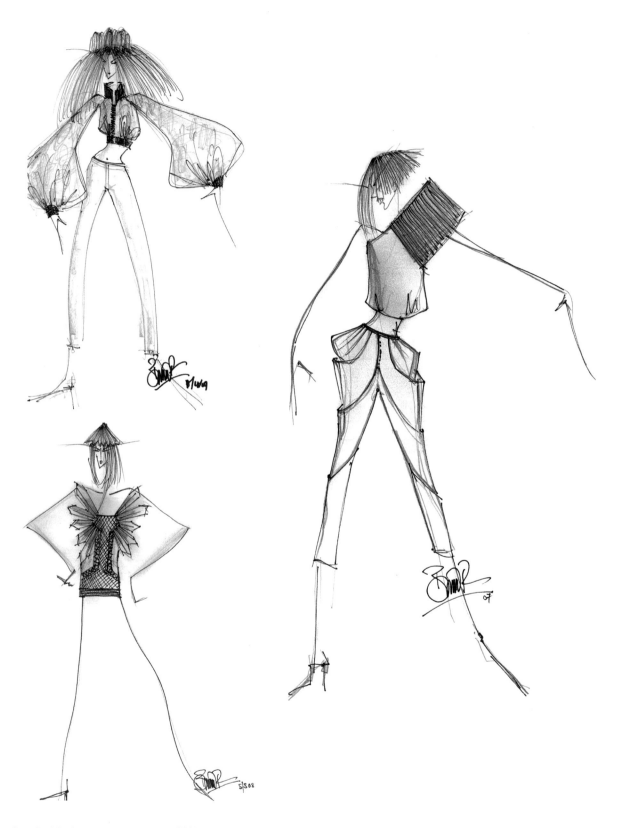

Sketches from the fall-winter and spring-summer 2008 collection

One garment

"The perfect
dress."

Sketch from the fall-winter 2007-2008 collection

One dream

"The satisfaction of a woman in my clothes."

Sketches from the fall-winter 2007-2008 collection

Sketches from the spring-summer 2007 and spring-summer-2008 collections

Sketch from the spring-summer 2008 collection

Betsey Johnson

www.betseyjohnson.com

One inspiration

"Grandchildren and family."

Betsey Johnson was born in Hartford, Connecticut. She studied at the Pratt Institute in New York and graduated from the Syracuse University in 1964. That year she was the director of the summer edition of the magazine *Mademoiselle*, where they then contracted her for a year. During this period, she took advantage of her free time to create fashion designs and sell them. Soon after she became an independent designer and managed to sell her garments in Paraphernalia, a New York period fashion boutique.

During the seventies, Johnson triumphed with a "transgressor designer" title by creating gangster-style striped suits, a vinyl dress that was sold with stars as adornments so that the wearer can fasten them wherever they wanted, a loud knit dress with loose rings sewn to the hem, silver motorist suits, tight-fitting jersey dresses, and a leather minidress to be worn with thigh-high leather boots.

In 1969, she opened a boutique in New York called Betsey Bunki Nini. In the seventies, Johnson devoted her time to designing disco wear, creating extravagant elastic garments, and in 1978 she launched a line of sportswear. In 2003 the Council of Fashion Designers of America named her an honorary chairwoman of the Fashion Targets Breast Cancer initiative, a project in which she is very involved.

Sketches of Leopard (left) and Tuesday (right)
swimwear from the spring-summer 2008 collection

"My sixties
paraphernalia
long, three-tiered
voile Spanish
Flamenco dress."

Sketch of the Ballerina dress from the spring-summer 2008 collection

Picture of the Ballerina dress from the spring-summer 2008 collection runway show

One dream

"For us all to share a happy and healthy planet."

Picture from the spring-summer 2008 collection runway show

Picture from the spring-summer 2008 collection runway show

Picture from the spring-summer 2008 collection runway show

Picture from the spring-summer 2008 collection runway show

Sketches from the fall-winter 2006-2007 collection

Bora Aksu

www.boraaksu.com

One inspiration

"It's mainly my friends who surround me. To start a collection, I always start out with something very personal like childhood reminiscences."

Bora Aksu, who is of Turkish origin but now established in London, graduated with honors and a masters degree in fashion design from in the Central Saint Martins College of Art & Design. Some of his first designs were purchased by Dolce & Gabbana, who gave him great inspiration and this first foray into fashion, along with a sponsorship to create his own label—what he needed to make his debut during the 2003 London Fashion Week.

Since then, he has become one of the benchmark designers of modern British fashion. His garments are characterized by the use of sophisticated cuts inspired by past eras, colors such as dark pink, black, gray or yellow, and pearl accessories. In partnership with Converse, he became one of the first designers to link couture with sportswear.

Bora works with different scenic arts entities such as the dance company Cathy Marston Project, for which he designed the wardrobe, and he has taken part in designing movie costumes such as those worn in *Troy* and *King Arthur*. Aksu has been awarded a Topshop New Generation sponsorship on four occasions. He has also received a young designer award from the British Fashion Council.

Sketch from the fall-winter 2006-2007 collection

Sketch from the fall-winter 2006-2007 collection

One garment

"Madeleine Vionnet dresses that still remain timeless."

Sketches from the fall-winter 2006-2007 collection

"When you are a student, you work in such a spirit that nothing really discourages you regarding the creativity. I always believe in keeping the amateur spirit within my work. I guess that's my aim to be able to carry on my work keeping the spirit of amateurism."

Sketch from the fall-winter 2006-2007 collection

Sketch from the fall-winter 2006-2007 collection

Sketches from the spring-summer 2008 collection

Carmen March

www.carmenmarch.com

Photo by Gonzalo Machado

One inspiration

"Anything I like."

Carmen March was born in Palma de Mallorca, Spain in 1974. She studied geography and history at the Universidad Complutense de Madrid before she enrolled a fashion design program at the Institude de Artes Visuais. She worked with Duyos & Paniagua and Javier Larrainzar for three years, up to 2000, when she opened Egotherapy along with Juanjo Oliva. From that year on, she designed her own collections in her workshop in Madrid, Núñez de Balboa street.

In 2004, Carmen had her first fashion show in the FEM (Madrid Edition Festival) and from then on began to present her collections at the Pasarela Gaudí in Barcelona. In September 2005, she made her debut at the Pasarela Cibeles, and that same year *Glamour* magazine named her Spain's best national designer. The next year she received the L'Oréal prize for the best spring-summer collection 2007 and the *Marie Claire* award for the best new Spanish designer in 2006.

Carmen became a member of the Spanish Association of Fashion Designers (ACME) in June 2007. Among her new projects are the opening of a new space located on Puigcerdá street in Madrid, and the designing of her first prêt-à-porter collection. Her garments regularly grace the fashion pages of magazines such as: *Vogue*, *Glamour*, *Vanity Fair*, *Telva*, *Marie Claire*, *Elle* and *Vanity*.

Sketch from the fall-winter 2007-2008 collection

One garment

"A coat."

Sketches from the fall-winter 2007-2008 collection

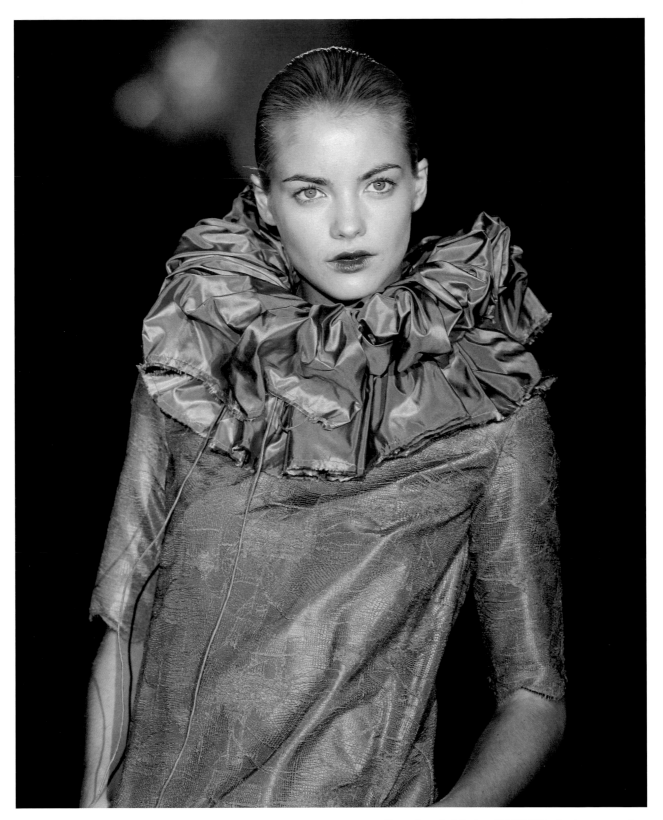

Picture from the fall-winter 2007-2008 collection runway show

One dream

"A fashion show in New York."

Picture from the fall-winter 2008-2009 collection runway show

Pictures from the spring-summer 2008 collection

Picture from the fall-winter 2008-2009 collection runway show

Picture from the fall-winter 2007-2008 collection runway show

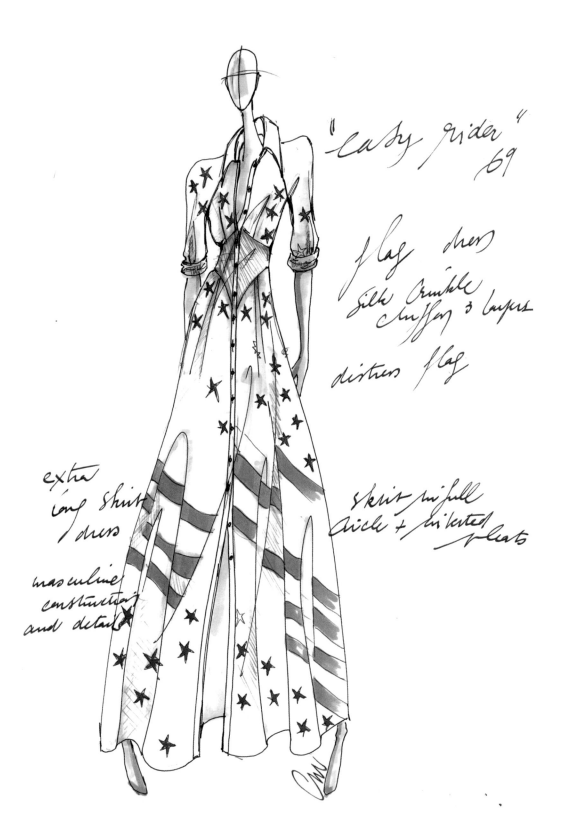

"easy rider" 69

flag dress
silk crinkle
chiffon 3 layers

distress flag

extra
long shirt
dress

masculine
construction
and details

skirt in full
circle + inverted
pleats

Sketch from the spring-summer 2007 collection

Catherine Malandrino

www.catherinemalandrino.com

One inspiration

"Contrasts—from Peter Fonda's attitude in Easy Rider and Death in Venice, an embroidered handkerchief, a wood carving sculpture, Maria Callas, Tina Turner, a piece of metal…"

The fashion designer Catherine Malandrino was born in Grenoble, France, and began her career in Paris working for international designers such as Emanuel Ungaro and Louis Féraud. In 1990, she played a part in the relaunch of the label Et Vous. In 1998, she moved to New York where she joined the Diane von Furstenberg label as head of design.

Since the creation of her own label, all Malandrino's designs have the perfect symbiosis between the energy of Manhattan and the Romanticism of Paris. For Malandrino, individuality is central to fashion. Each woman is different; and for this reason her collections emphasize eclecticism. In 2002, the designer launched the Catherine Malandrino Limited Edition collection, which consists of designs made up from exclusively-distributed unique garments. Iconic pieces include a daytime raincoat and a pleated cocktail dress. In 2006, she launched her first accessory collection, which included shoes and bags.

Her most loyal fans include Madonna, Sarah Jessica Parker, Cameron Diaz, Halle Berry, Winona Ryder and Julia Roberts. Both the Catherine Malandrino collection and the Catherine Malandrino Limited Edition collection are sold internationally in the USA, Japan, UK, Hong Kong, Singapore, Germany, France, and Italy.

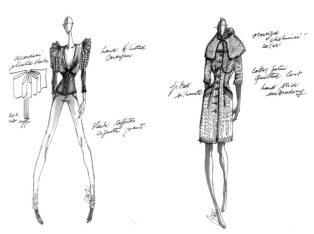

Sketches from the spring-summer 2007 collection

One garment

"Any from the first moment when your sketches become a reality, and 'giving birth' to my designs by draping, cutting, the shearing."

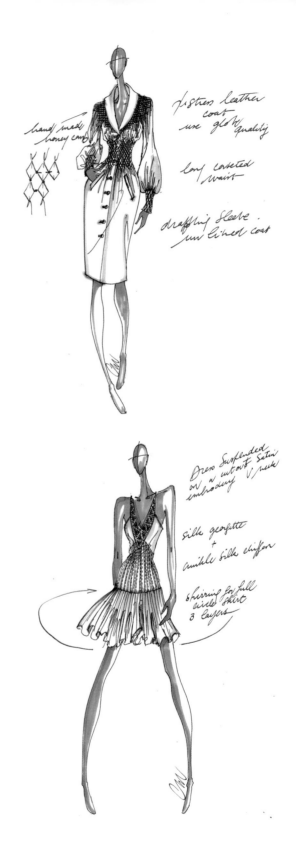

Sketches from the spring-summer 2007 collection

"Redefining the home through a maison hotel that would propose a different approach to life for the women that I am dressing."

Oversized knit dress strok yarn

open pointelle 16 g 2 pl geometric pattern

drapping sleeve

long macramé cuff

Sketch from the spring-summer 2007 collection

Sketchbooks from the spring-summer 2007 collection

Cecilia Sörensen

www.ceciliasorensen.com

One inspiration

One inspiration

"My family, my partner, my friends, my dog, all the rooms I have ever lived in, my books, my dreams, my memories, the documental photograph from the beginning of the century such as the photograph of August Sander."

Born in Helsinki, Cecilia graduated in fashion design in 2001 in Barcelona, a degree she had started in the UK. Her training included studying patterns in Helsinki and working with the designer Antonio Miró. In 2002, she won the award for the Best Young Designer granted by ModaFAD Barcelona.

Since then, Cecilia has become part of the designers group Comité. The group's headquarters is in Barcelona and it has very singular characteristics, with all members agreeing when it comes to decisions on intimacy, detail, quality and subtlety. The young designer is also co-owner of the Bingo Shop in Barcelona.

Sörensen's approach to design is based on unique pieces and locally and ethically produced collections, which will be the only way to offer the buyer luxury in the near future. "The type of clientele that I want, are those who seek a special type of quality," she said.

Cecilia has presented her collection at fashion shows several times, and she is also a regular in fairs such as Bread & Butter and the Rendez-Vous. Currently, the designer offers two lines of fashion: an all female collection, Cecilia Sörensen, and Pequeños Héroes, a collection made from recycled material. Her collections are sold in Spain, Sweden, France, Italy, Germany, and Japan.

Sketchbook from the spring-summer 2007 collection

One garment

"Oversized t-shirts with small buttons."

Sketchbooks from the spring-summer 2007 collection

Sketchbooks from the spring-summer 2007 collection

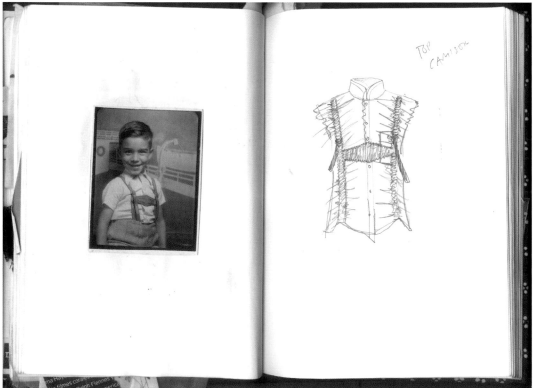

Sketchbooks from the spring-summer 2007 collection

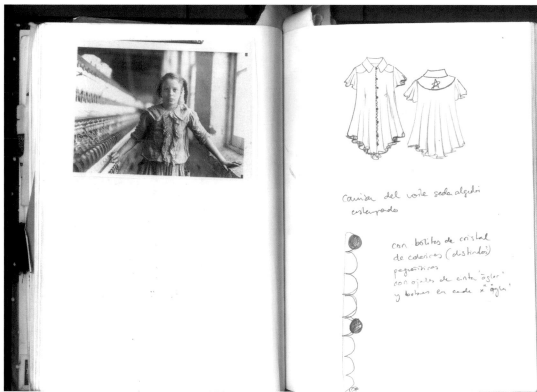

Sketchbooks from the spring-summer 2007 collection

Picture of fall-winter 2008-2009 collection. Photo by Paul Mpagi Sepu

Claudia
Rosa Lukas

www.lukas-by.com

Photo by Sebastian Toth

One inspiration

"My social environment."

Claudia Rosa Lukas is a young Vienna-based Austrian designer. She completed her studies at the University of Applied Arts in Vienna and HdK (now the University of the Arts) in Berlin in 1997, during which time she had figures such as Vivienne Westwood, Helmut Lang, Marc Bohan, and Jean Charles de Castelbajac as professors. She started her own fashion business shortly after graduating.

In 2002, she took part in the Enkamania competition in Italy, chaired by Franca Sozzani, who subsequently supported her participation in the European Commission's EU Gateway to Japan project, that was presenting a taste of European design and fashion to the Japanese public.

Lukas produces collections that embody her creative expression through minimalist designs, pieces featuring structured cuts and forms with sensuality and persuasion. The choice of fabric is limited by function and wearability, which is why her designs make use of Austrian and Italian wools, jerseys, and cottons.

Lukas shows special interest in taking part in different multimedia and costume design projects. Her clothes have appeared in the pages of fashion magazines such as *ID*, *Oyster* and *Tiger*. The designer presents her collections during the Paris Prêt-à-Porter Fashion Week and at fashion fairs in France and Italy. Her designs are sold in Austria, France, and Japan.

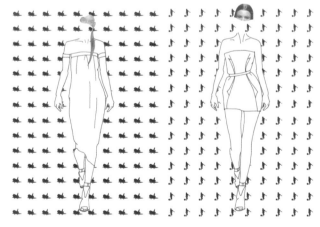

Sketches from the spring-summer 2008 collection

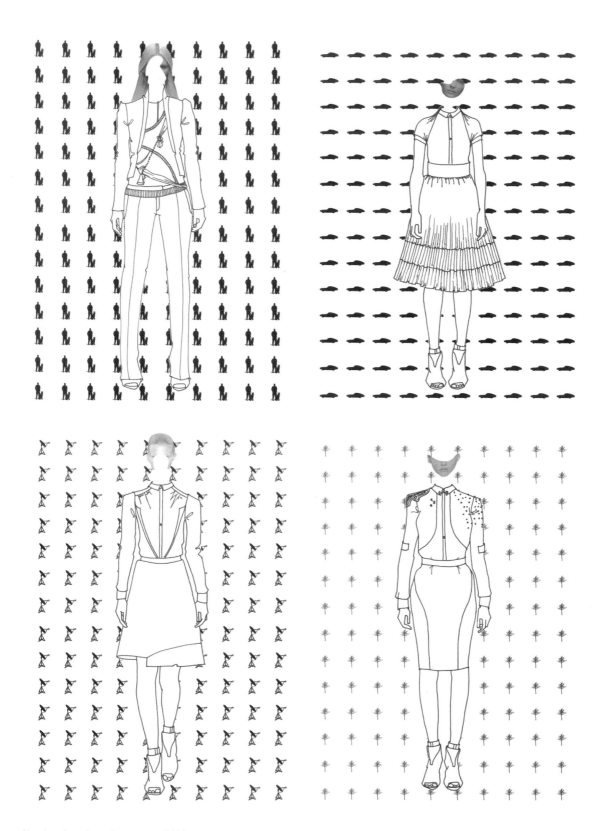

Sketches from the spring-summer 2008 collection

One garment

"A trench coat."

Picture of the fall-winter 2008-2009 campaign. Photo by Paul Mpagi Sepu

One dream

"Amor Vincit Omnia by Caravaggio."

Pictures from the spring-summer 2008 collection. Photos by Katharina Gossow

Picture from the spring-summer 2007 collection. Photo by Gregor Titze

Picture from the fall-winter 2006-2007 campaign

Comentrigo

www.comentrigo.com

One inspiration

"Improvisation."

The Spanish Comentrigo label was founded by the design duo Aura Chavarria and Elena Maggi. The union of two different personalities and styles result in a wide variety of subtle looks combining opposites such as masculine with feminine and simplicity with complexity. Their first collection was for spring-summer 2006 and was given the name Storytellers. It was an opportunity for them to present their fresh and dreamy style and love of embroidery, lace, padded looks, and retro fabrics.

They often turn to nature, from the sea to botany, as inspiration for their collections, and they make use of muted colors. Their favorites include neutral tones—black, gray, white—and "non-colors" like nude or flesh tone, and very light makeup bordering on pallid. The result is a series of pieces with very feminine cuts and volume and with a touch of fantasy and playfulness.

Comentrigo is currently one of the highest profile labels on the Spanish fashion scene. Their collections are shown at the Pasarela Barcelona Fashion Week, and their designs are regularly featured in international magazines such as *Marie Claire*, *Vogue* and *Glamour*. Their clothes are on sale in Barcelona, Madrid, and Tokyo.

Picture of the spring-summer 2008 campaign

One garment

"A dress."

Sketches from the spring-summer 2009 collection (above) and inspirations for the spring-summer 2009 collection (below)

Pictures from the spring-summer 2008 campaign

One dream

"Continuing to design following our own ideals."

Ron Brugal contest picture

Picture from the spring-summer 2008 campaign

31
JADE

Sketch from the spring-summer 2007 collection

Corinne Cobson

www.corinnecobson.com

One inspiration

"A pair of legs walking in the street, at a coffee-terrace where images pass by, images flowing (clips, pictures, films)."

Corinne Cobson has been linked to the world of fashion since she was a child, when her family owned a clothing store. She created her own line when she was very young, and from her first fashion show, her rebellious, nonconformist and impulsive character was clear. She has worked for labels such as Cacharel, Monoprix, Alain Mikli, Variance, and L'Oréal. From the start, some of her outfits were highly successful such as a satin-finish black dress or a pair of jeans combined with a leather jacket, pieces that have become signatures in her collections, and which she continuously reinterprets.

Corinne's collections are inspired by her travels around the world. Visionary and with immense sensitivity for all that originates from the world of art and culture, her imagination is fed on photography and cinema. Along with her husband, moviemaker Tanguy Loyzance, and with influences such as John Cassavetes, she has made a short movie in which her clothes play an important role and take on life thanks to the characters that she dresses.

In her Paris boutique, Corinne has created, alongside Sam Baron, a multimedia space that holds activities linked to the cinema, acts, concerts, exhibitions, poetry and video-art sessions. Celebrities such as Vanessa Paradis, Mathilde Seigner, Virginie Ledoyen, Cécile Cassel and Mélanie Lauren are among her clientele.

Sketches from the spring-summer 2007 collection

20
LAURIE

30
LAURIE

37
LAURIE

47
LAURIE

Sketches from the spring-summer 2007 collection

21
KATI

One garment

"A fetish
Corinne Cobson
leather jacket
that I have since
1992 and wear
every day."

52 CARMEN

53 CLAIRE

54 SHANA

60 SYBIL

Sketches from the spring-summer 2007 collection

61
NAOMI

Sketch from the spring-summer 2007 collection

Corinne Cobson 171

One dream

"A bakery. It represents for me happiness, poetry, perfumes. To me a good baker is a real artist."

Sketches from the spring-summer 2007 collection

SyBiL

Sketch from the spring-summer 2007 collection

Corinne Cobson 173

Picture from the spring-summer 2007 collection runway show

Costume National

www.costumenational.com

One inspiration

"My wife, Dragana."

Born in the Italian region of Puglia, Ennio Capasa showed a special passion for the Eastern culture from a young age. As an eighteen-year-old, he traveled to Japan before he enrolled in the Brera Academy of Fine Arts in Milan, where he studied sculpture. After graduating, Capasa returned to Japan and formed part of Yohji Yamamoto's team after Yamamoto saw sketches Capasa had sent to a friend.

In 1987, the designer returned to Milan and created the label Costume National with his brother Carlo, who had worked with Romeo Gigli and as Dawn Mello's advisor in Gucci. His first collection offered clothing designs and a line of Japanese inspired shoes. However, the pure and minimalist style of the Capasa brothers was not well received in Milan. In 1991, they decided to move to Paris along with Yamamoto and Rei Kawakubo.

In 1993, they added a male line and another line of shoes. In 2000, they added bags, lingerie, and the Costume National Luxe line, a limited edition collection of articles conceived with unusual materials and designs. In 2002, they launched their first perfume and later a line of eyewear.

Currently, Costume National shoes takes up a third of their business volume. Costume National has its own factory in Padua and stores in Milan, Paris, New York, Los Angeles, Tokyo, Osaka and Hong Kong.

Moodboard (2008)

Sketches from the spring-summer 2007 (above) and the fall-winter 2008-2009 collections (below)

One garment

"A black dress worn with high heels."

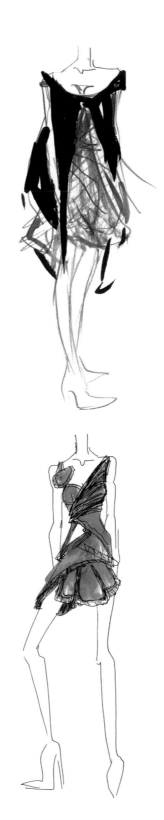

EGUE
SERAZ

D
TCH

BODY
819

VOLUME
MANITA
V 810
5 cm
+ COUTI

Sketches from the fall-winter 2008-2009 collection

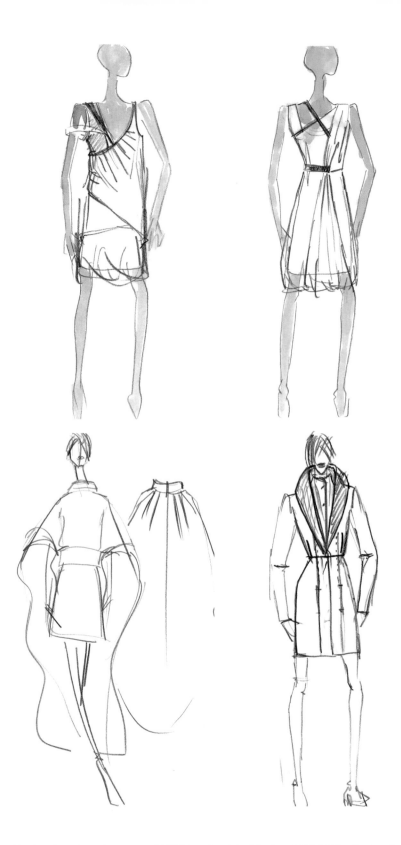

One dream

"To keep doing what I like to do."

Sketches from the spring-summer 2007 (above) and the fall-winter 2008-2009 collections (below)

Pictures from the fall-winter 2008-2009 collection runway show

Illustration (2007)

Daniel
Herman

www.danielherman.com

One inspiration

"Female body."

Born in Switzerland, the designer Daniel Herman studied in Central Saint Martins and graduated in 1998. Soon after, he was offered the opportunity to work as John Galliano's assistant. Two years later and after gaining enough experience, he embarked on his personal adventure with the launch of his own label in Zurich.

After winning the prestigious Swiss Textiles Award in 2000, he presented his first collection during the London Fashion Week for the 2002 season. As an independent designer, Daniel has worked with different textile and fashion companies such as Jakob Schläpfer, Akris and Sharon Wauchob. Daniel Herman has been a design consultant for Gessner for a few years and has worked with Triumph International, creating three special collections per year. In 2005, he also began to work as a consultant for Micalady.

Herman's work shows his interest in lingerie and textile development. He is up-to-date with new technologies and he applies the most cutting-edge techniques in the entire clothing production process.

Since 2003, his work has frequently appeared in the main fashion international publications such as *Vogue*, *Marie Claire*, *Surface*, *Above* and *V Magazine*. His clothes can be bought in multi-brand establishments in Europe and Japan as well as from his website www.strippedandwhipped.com.

Illustration for flyer (2007)

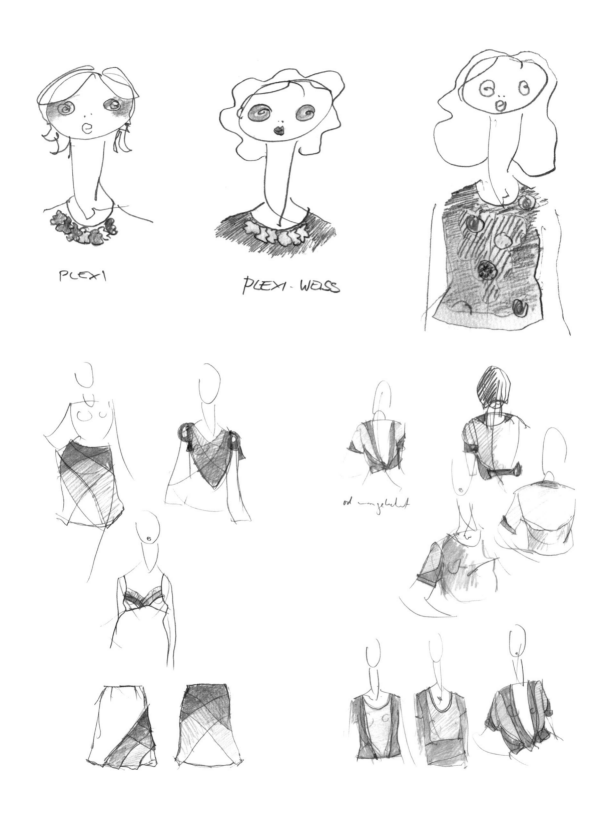

PLEXI

PLEXI-WEISS

Prêt-à-porter and lingerie 2008 collection sketches

One garment

"Underwear, because of the need to condensate ideas."

Prêt-à-porter and lingerie 2008 collection sketches

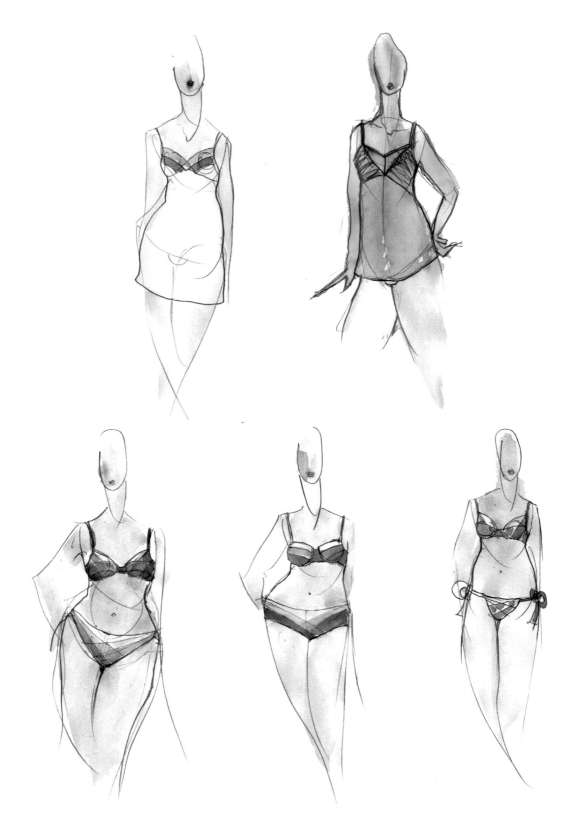

Prêt-à-porter and lingerie 2008 collection sketches

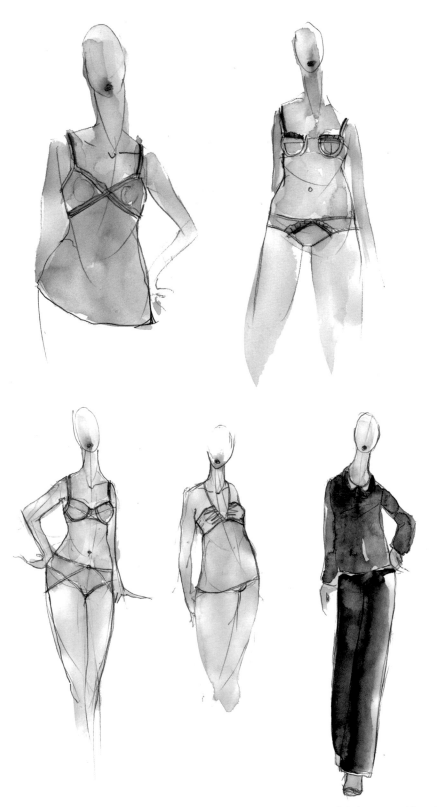

Prêt-à-porter and lingerie 2008 collection sketches

One dream

"Finding more time to paint."

Above and below left: pictures from the Latex campaign fall-winter collection 2006-2007. Photos by Stefan Schacher
Below right: laser-cut detail from the spring-summer collection 2004. Photo by Tom Dura

Picture of the Daniel Herman campaign for Triumph, spring-summer 2004 collection. Photo by Andrea Diglas

Sketches from the fall-winter 2007-2008 collection

Disaya

www.disaya.com

One inspiration

"My inspiration is my family and the people I love. I use beautiful things which I see everyday and try and turn them into something wearable which people will always be curious about."

Born in Thailand, Disaya Prakobsantisukh moved to the UK in 1997 to study design in Central Saint Martins. In 2002, after graduating, she won the L'Oréal Professional Total Look Award. Disaya formed part of the John Galliano design team in Paris, but she decided to return to London to complete her studies for a masters, for which she received a special mention.

In 2004 she won the Lancôme Color Designs Award. The Italian designer Alberta Ferretti, impressed by Disaya's work, offered her the opportunity to join her company, but Disaya refused the offer to return to Thailand and create her own label, Boudoir. Her label offers delicate textiles such as cotton, silk, chiffon, angora or cashmere in colors ranging from purple, red, and midnight blue to metallic shades. Boudoir is a line of clothing and jewelry aimed at the daring and dynamic teenager or the more sophisticated mature lady who looks for that touch of subtle luxury.

Disaya's most famous fans are Jennifer Lopez, Kelly Osbourne, Amy Winehouse and Agyness Deyn. Her collections are sold in over twenty countries in prestigious establishments such as Henri Bendel, Le Bon Marché, Seibu, Harrods, and Harvey Nichols.

Sketches from the fall-winter 2007-2008 collection

Sketches from the fall-winter 2007-2008 collection

One garment

"I love my corset style dresses. They look beautiful on everyone and so unique."

Sketch from the fall-winter 2007-2008 collection

"My dream is to make women feel fabulous and comfortable in my clothes. One assumes that if you buy it you feel confident, but I just want people to feel that extra special safety blanket around them."

Sketches from the fall-winter 2007-2008 collection

Sketch from the fall-winter 2007-2008 collection

Sketches from the fall-winter 2005-2006 campaign

Duckie Brown

www.duckiebrown.com

One inspiration

"Our inspiration is always the same—the life we lead. Duckie Brown evolves organically each season. A new collection starts where the last one left off."

Daniel Silver and Steven Cox founded Duckie Brown in New York with the idea of reviewing classic male design patterns and offering a new focus. They created the label in 2002, and from the start they have shown a special passion for daring colors, unusual fabrics, sequins and embroidery, elements that until then were unusual in male collections.

Duckie Brown distribution is limited, owing to the individuality of the garments, but its clientele list is impressive. Currently, Daniel and Steven work with Florsheim, for whom they design a small collection of dress shoes with eccentric, but not extravagant, colors. In their latest designs, the duo has focused on fabrics such as cotton or nylon for raincoats that appear to be rigid but are actually hardwearing—like those of the older days, bomber style jackets and anoraks. Organza is used for an ivory-colored blazer and for suits that perfectly adjust to the body. Other unusual elements in their collections are leotards and tight gloves.

In 2007, Daniel and Steven won the award for Best Male Designers by the Council of Fashion Designers of America. Their garments appear in male fashion magazines such as *Esquire*, *GQ* and *Vogue Uomo* and are sold in the USA.

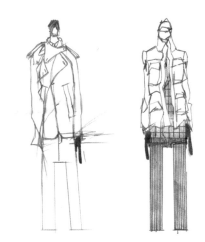

Sketches from the fall-winter 2005-2006 campaign

One garment

"It's always about the tailored jacket for us. Each collection starts with the shoulder and works out from there. We love jackets, tailored jackets, beautiful jackets."

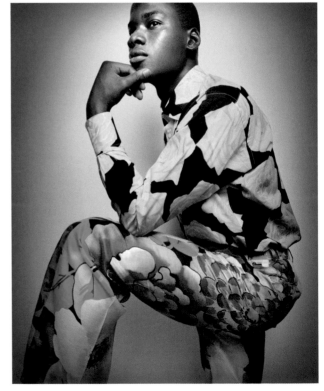

Above: picture from the spring-summer 2008 campaign
Below: pictures from the fall-winter 2005-2006 campaign (left) and the spring-summer 2008 campaign (right)

Picture from the fall-winter 2005-2006 campaign

Picture from the fall-winter 2005-2006 campaign

One dream

"We are living our dream. We get to design and produce beautiful clothing for people. Every day, we wake up and say how lucky we are."

Picture from the spring-summer 2008 collection runway show

One garment

"My garment of choice would be a double-breasted jacket with a long rolling lapel, high arm-holes and a wider lapel, waisted and slightly flared."

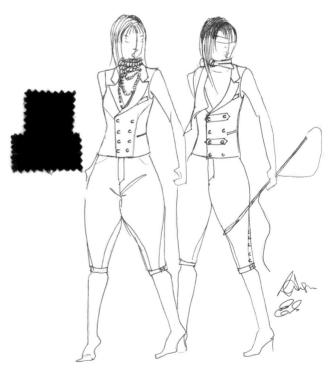

Sketches from the winter 2006-2007 collection

"My dream from
the day we started
has been to set
trends as opposed
to following them.
Translating what
we do for our
private clients to a
broader audience
by way of a ready-
to-wear collection."

Sketch from the winter 2006-2007 collection

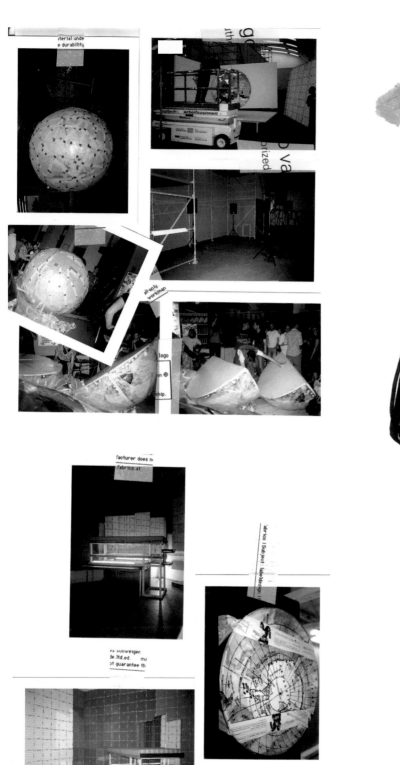

Artwork and sketch from the spring-summer 2007 collection

Fabrics
Interseason

www.fabrics.at

Photo by Sybille Walter

One inspiration

"Asphalt and accidentism."

Austrian designers Wally Salner and Johannes Schweiger are the brains behind the Fabrics Interseason label. This project has surfaced from these young designers' passion, not only for fashion, but also for fine arts, history, music, and electronics. Their collections emerge from this combination of elements and from the partnership of professionals linked to the world of art.

This label has ignored the traditional methods of formal design and maintained their company as a private company based on a unique spirit. The creative duo is especially interested in the codes that reflect the thought behind each garment: the combination of the technical structure and sensorial perceptions. The choice of materials and the refined silhouettes provide garments designed for an urban public with simple cuts and energetic patterns of different types that make references to graphic design, to artistic movements and to society.

The Fabrics Interseason collections have a very solid base and are well-respected among the most innovative designers. They are presented twice a year at the Paris Fashion Weeks. Their clothes can be found in select establishments in Europe, Asia and Australia.

Sketch from the spring-summer 2007 collection

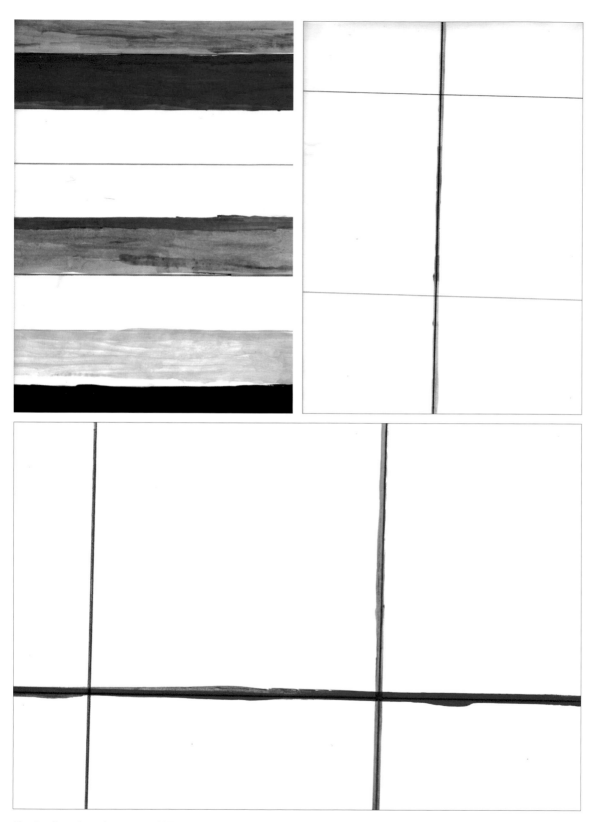

Sketches from the spring-summer 2007 collection

One garment

"Cotton."

Pictures from the Heitzing Reform fall-winter 2008-2009 collection

One dream

"Satisfaction, composure."

Picture from the Heitzing Reform fall-winter 2008-2009 collection

Sketch from the eveningwear and cocktail dress fall-winter 2006-2007 collection

Fátima
Lopes

www.fatima-lopes.com

One inspiration

"Life."

Fátima Lopes, a self-taught Portuguese designer, started her career after moving from Madeira to Lisbon, the city where she opened her famous Versus store. A few years later, she embarked on her most creative adventure: traveling for more than two years to gather inspirations to express in her creations.

The result of her travels is a series of original collections in which ethnic and mixed influences are evident. During this period, Fátima produced her famous Moroccan-inspired line of bags and accessories. In 1999, she presented her first fashion show during Paris Fashion Week. Both a business woman and an endless creator, she designed her own networks of franchises in 2000 and in 2005 she started her career as a fine jewelry designer with her collection Fátima Lopes Diamond. The collection is a line conceived by the recognized jeweler Pedro Rosas. It is a collection of refined pieces that use diamonds as a base material.

In February 2006, Fátima was awarded the title of Comendadora da Ordem do Infante D. Henrique by the President of Portugal at that time, Jorge Sampaio. Her latest creative adventures involve the world of decor. Today Fátima presents her collections in Paris.

Sketches from the eveningwear and cocktail dress fall-winter 2006-2007 collection

Sketches from the eveningwear and cocktail dress fall-winter 2006-2007 collection

One garment

"My gold
and diamond
bikini."

Sketch from the eveningwear and cocktail dress fall-winter 2006-2007 collection

"To keep on designing new collections."

Sketches from the eveningwear and cocktail dresses fall-winter 2006-2007 collection

Sketches from the eveningwear and cocktail dress fall-winter 2006-2007 collection

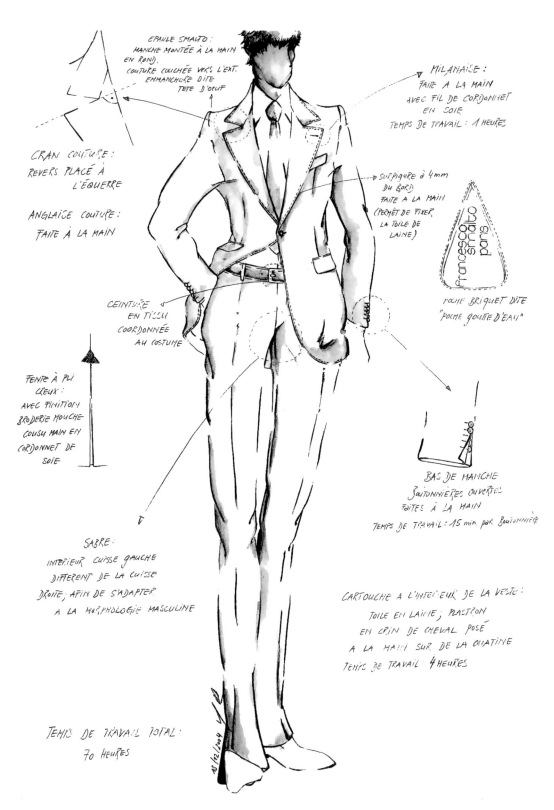

ÉPAULE SMALTO:
MANCHE MONTÉE À LA MAIN
EN ROND.
COUTURE COUCHÉE VERS L'EXT.
EMMANCHURE DITE
TÊTE D'ŒUF

MILANAISE:
FAITE À LA MAIN
AVEC FIL DE CORDONNET
EN SOIE
TEMPS DE TRAVAIL: 1 HEURES

CRAN COUTURE:
REVERS PLACÉ À
L'ÉQUERRE

ANGLAISE COUTURE:
FAITE À LA MAIN

SURPIQÛRE à 4mm
DU BORD
FAITE À LA MAIN
(PERMET DE FIXER
LA TOILE DE
LAINE)

POCHE BRIQUET DITE
"POCHE GOUTTE D'EAU"

CEINTURE
EN TISSU
COORDONNÉE
AU COSTUME

FENTE À PLI
CREUX:
AVEC FINITION
BRODERIE MOUCHE
COUSU MAIN EN
CORDONNET DE
SOIE

BAS DE MANCHE
BOUTONNIÈRES OUVERTES
FAITES À LA MAIN
TEMPS DE TRAVAIL: 15 min. PAR BOUTONNIÈRE

SABRE:
INTÉRIEUR CUISSE GAUCHE
DIFFÉRENT DE LA CUISSE
DROITE, AFIN DE S'ADAPTER
A LA MORPHOLOGIE MASCULINE

CARTOUCHE A L'INTÉRIEUR DE LA VESTE:
TOILE EN LAINE; PLASTRON
EN CRIN DE CHEVAL POSÉ
A LA MAIN SUR DE LA OUATINE
TEMPS DE TRAVAIL 4 HEURES

TEMPS DE TRAVAIL TOTAL:
70 HEURES

Sketch from the fall-winter 2006-2007 collection

Francesco Smalto

www.smalto.com

"My open attitude to the world."

Since 1962, the year the label was created, Francesco Smalto has featured at the top of lists linked to haute couture. Suits that adapt to the body as if they were tailor-made has been the theme of this label from its beginnings and the milestone that marked fashion of the seventies. The company's iconic designs include the vinyl boots worn by the first astronauts who walked on the Moon, as well as costumes for several cinema productions. In 1970, the first Francesco Smalto boutique opened in Paris.

Youn Chong Bak is in charge of the company's design area. When she joined, the brand was known for its own traditional tailored style. Her challenge was to expand on this concept, and the result was a wide range of accessories and a second line of more casual wear. The company's constant search for the best materials and an evolution in their cut, allows them to offer garments made from a unique mix of fabrics such as wool or silver fox, which are highly enjoyed by the British.

Since 2003, the company has belonged to Alliance Designers who maintain the spirit of a label linked to high quality couture and to the constant evolution regarding design. They have points of sale all over the world, and all the main fashion magazines praise its hands on approach to the world of fashion and retail.

Picture of the Francesco Smalto atelier

One garment

"A man's suit."

Sketches from the fall-winter 2006-2007 collection

"Getting a brand environment focusing on luxurious but contemporary elegance."

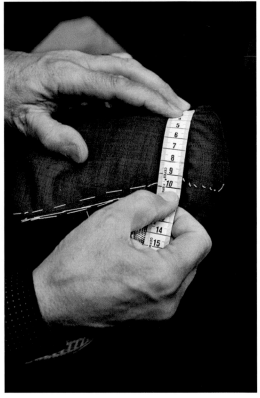

Pictures of the Francesco Smalto atelier

Picture of the Francesco Smalto atelier

Pictures from the fall-winter 2006-2007 collection runway show

Twisted shirt
dress

Stretch
cotton faille
in bias

I

Sketch from the fall-winter 2006-2007 campaign

Gilles Rosier

info@gillesrosier.fr

One inspiration

"Contemporary choreography, movement, attitude, gesture...and traditional tailoring."

Born in Paris in 1961 to a French father and a German mother, Gilles Rosier frequently moved around as a child. He lived in Algiers, Port-Gentil and Kinshasa. When he returned to Paris, Rosier had gained enough knowledge to draw from a global perspective. He studied in the Chambre Syndicale de la Haute Couture, where he graduated in 1982. After carrying out a worthwhile apprenticeship with Pierre Balmain and Christian Dior, he joined forces with Guy Paulin.

In 1987, Gilles worked with Jean Paul Gaultier and five years later he presented his first masculine collection for Léonard. This same year Rosier created and oversaw his own label, a task that he performed while simultenously working for Lacoste for seven years. His years in Kenzo as creative director earned him definitive recognition: between 1998 and 2003 he managed to recover its glamorous and sophisticated image with ostentatious garments.

With the help of Miroglio, Rosier moved to Milan to focus on his own label and develop collections based on the simplicity of lines and the use of neutral colors such as black, gray and white, and earth-based chromatic colors. In 2005, he added a male line to his collections. One of his favorite hobbies is working with theaters designing wardrobes for plays such as Chekhov's and Shakespeare's.

Pictures from the fall-winter 2006-2007 campaign

One garment

"Pieces that are supposed to be 'timeless'."

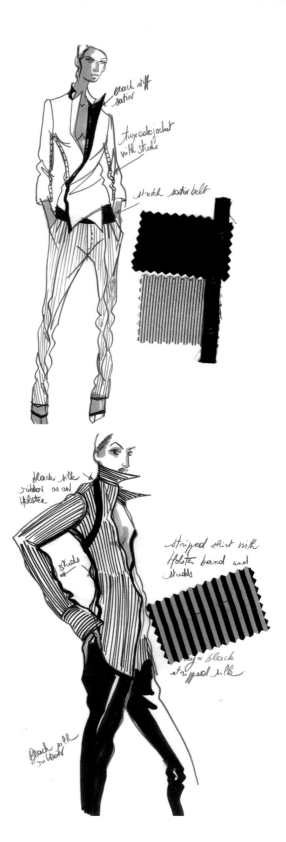

Sketches from the fall-winter 2006-2007 collection

Black elastic

Polka dots lurex chiffon

Black
grosgrain

One dream

"Getting better and better every season…"

Sketch from the fall-winter 2006-2007 collection

Sketches from the fall-winter 2007-2008 collection inspired by bondage

Gori de Palma

www.gorideplama.com

One inspiration

"Surrealism."

Since his appearance in 2004 at the Pasarela Gaudí, Gori de Palma has become one of the not-to-be-missed names of the new generation of Spanish designers. He was born in Mallorca in 1976, and his work has been characterized by a hard and blunt style as well as being both avant-garde and sophisticated. His unmistakable aesthetics are inspired by suburban movements such as punk and rock & roll as well as fetishistic imagery from bondage and sadomasochism movements—a subversive and provocative style that he works on through a visionary and personal concept of today's fashions.

Gori's dramatic career in the world of design and style has allowed him to carry out remarkable partnerships with musicians such as Calamaro, Sidonie and Pastora with *EP3* and MTV Italia involved, and with fashion labels such as Vans (MerkaFAD) and Wella, as well as punctual interventions in the world of art with Manuel Albarrán or the Museum of Contemporary Art of Castilla y León, and advertising with Garage Films, Sofa Experience Communications, and Nanouk Films.

In recent years, the label has launched two new partnerships with multi-nationals American Apparel, to design a collection of controversial T-shirts, and Swarovski, to launch an exclusive line of bags and cases.

Sketches from the fall-winter 2007-2008 collection inspired by bondage

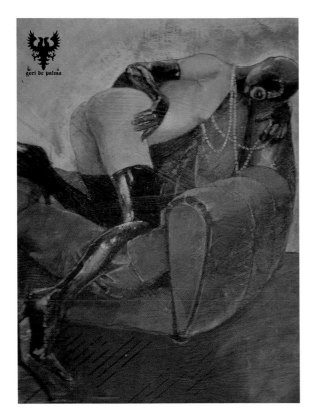

One garment

"T-shirt."

Sketches from the fall-winter 2007-2008 collection inspired by bondage

One dream

"To live on my profession."

Sketches from the spring-summer 2007 collection inspired by rock & roll and punk

Sketch from the fall-winter 2007-2008 collection

Guy Laroche

www.guylaroche.com

One inspiration

"Peter Greenaway, Alfred Hitchcock, and Luchino Visconti movies."

French designer Guy Laroche was born in 1923 in La Rochelle, France. He went to Paris at an early age to work in a hat shop. After the second World War he spent two years working on Seventh Avenue in New York. Then he returned to Paris to join the Jean Dessés design team, where he remained for eight years, until he set up on his own label in 1957. He started with haute couture, then in 1960 he designed his first prêt-à-porter line. His garments were characterized by impeccable tailoring and cuts.

After the death of Guy Laroche in 1987, several designers have taken over his label. Since 2007, Marcel Marongiu has served as the company's artistic director. Besides designing the female collection, he is in charge of supervising the eighty licenses in the Laroche universe around the world.

Born in Paris in 1962 to a French father and a Swedish mother, Marcel lived in Stockholm, where he studied economics, art and fashion. In 2003, he launched his first male collection. With a special gift for asymmetric lines, pleats and couture silhouettes, he was chosen for the Guy Laroche label because of his spirit, his culture, his technical capacities and his treatment of certain materials. His most loyal fans include Alicia Keys, Dido, Madonna, Isabelle Huppert, Neneh Cherry, and Emmanuelle Béart.

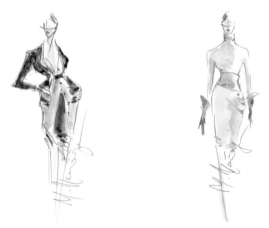

Sketches from the fall-winter 2007-2008 collection

One garment

"Knitted dresses."

Sketches from the fall-winter 2007-2008 collection

One dream

"To continue designing."

Picture from the fall-winter 2007-2008 collection runway show

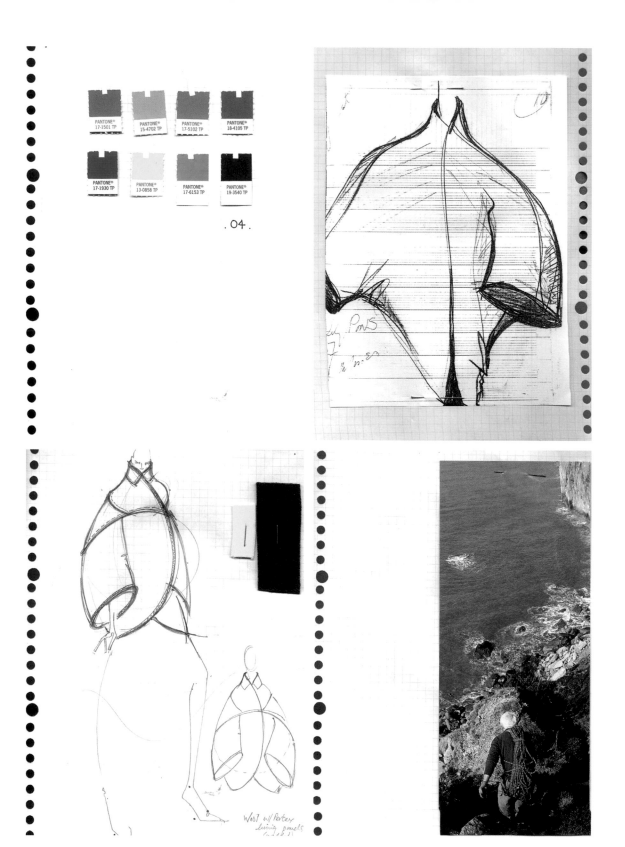

Sketchbooks from the fall-winter 2004-2005 collection

Hamish Morrow

www.hamishmorrow.com

Photo by Stefan Zeisler

One inspiration

"Technology."

In 1989, the South Africa-born Hamish Morrow moved to London where he studied fashion in Central Saint Martins. Due to economic problems, he had to drop out and began to work as a designer and pattern designer until he was able to afford to enroll in the Royal College of Art. There, Hamish earned a masters degree in male fashion and joined the Milan-based company Byblos. Later, he worked for other renowned international fashion houses such as Krizia, Fendi, and Louis Féraud in Paris.

In 2000, Hamish returned to the UK and set up his own company. The following year he presented his first fashion show during the London Fashion Week, entitled "The Life Cycle of an Idea," for which he received rave reviews. Since then, he has become a standard in avant-garde fashion thanks to collections in which music and art are a permanent source of inspiration and top quality fabrics, and defined cuts are a constant.

Hamish's collaboration with other fashion companies includes the creation of a special line for Topshop and a collection of denim and metallic fabric garments for Yoox.com. Although his creative study is located in London, he presents his collections during the Paris Fashion Week twice a year.

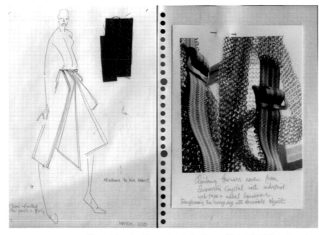

Sketchbooks from the fall-winter 2004-2005 collection

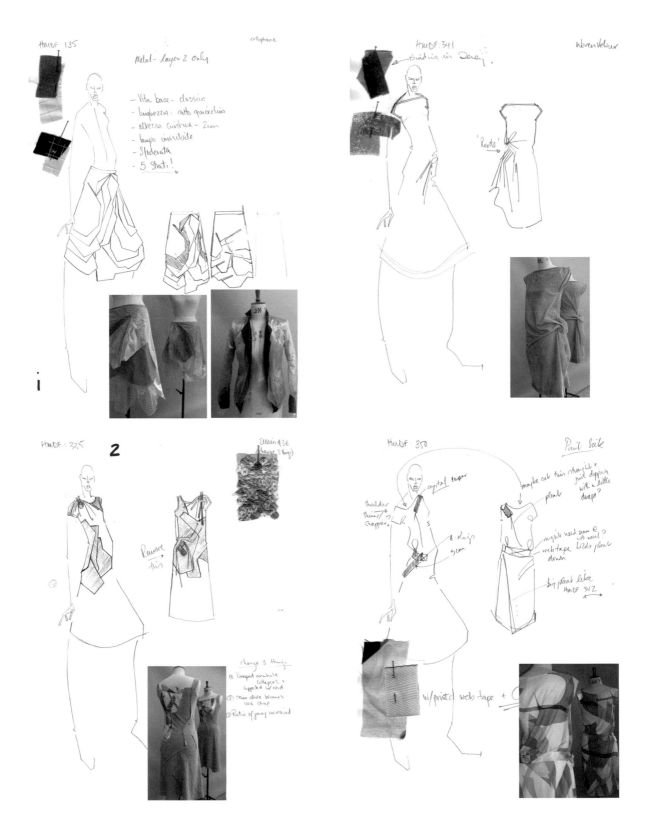

Sketches from the fall-winter 2004-2005 collection

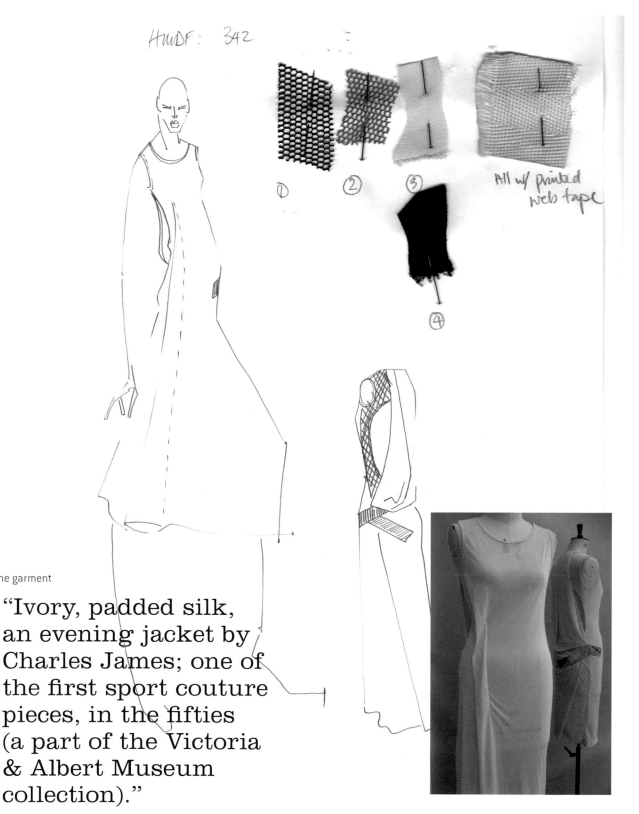

HMDF: 342

① ② ③

④

All w/ printed web tape

One garment

"Ivory, padded silk, an evening jacket by Charles James; one of the first sport couture pieces, in the fifties (a part of the Victoria & Albert Museum collection)."

Sketchbooks from the fall-winter 2004-2005 collection

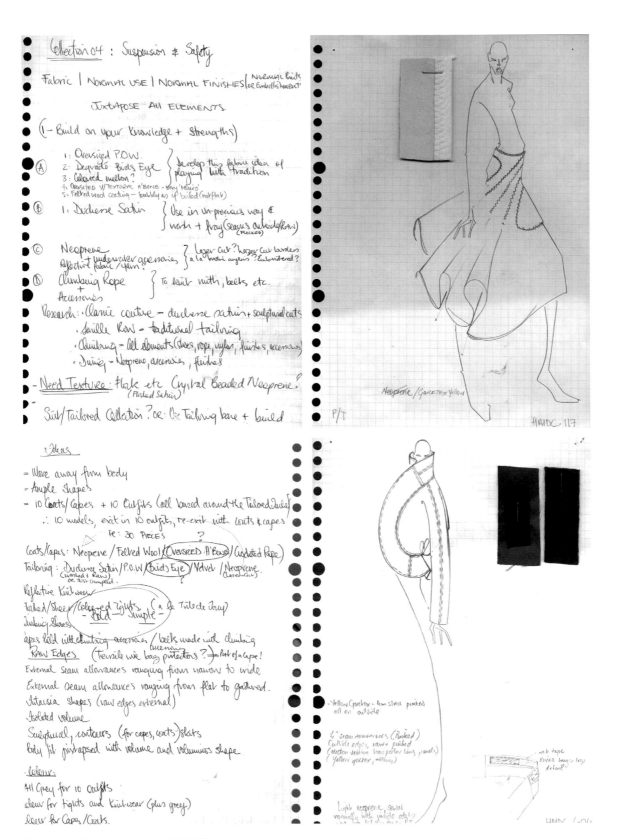

Collection 04: Suspension & Safety

Fabric | NORMAL USE | NORMAL FINISHES | Normal Prints or Embellishment

JUXTAPOSE ALL ELEMENTS.

(1 – Build on your Knowledge + Strengths)

(A)
1: Oversized P.O.W.
2: Degrade Birds Eye } Develop this fabric idea of
3: Coloured melton } playing with tradition
4: Oversized V/TEXTURAL H'BONE – very 'retro'
5: Felted wool coating – knobbly as if boiled (cork/flock)

(B)
1: Duchesse Satin } Use in un-precious way &
} work + fray (seams outside/Raw)
(PINKED)

(C) Neoprene } Laser Cut? Laser Cut borders
+ underwater accessories } a la 'maui angels'? Embroidered?
Reflective fabric / yarn

(D) Climbing Rope } To knit with, belts etc.
+
Accessories

Research: · Classic couture – duchesse satin + sculptural cuts
· Saville Row – traditional tailoring
· Climbing – All elements (shoes, rope, nylon, knits, accessories)
· Diving – Neoprene, accessories, finishes

– Need Texture: Flock etc Crystal Beaded Neoprene?
(Pinked Satin)

· Suit/Tailored Collection? OR: Use Tailoring base + build

Neoprene / GORETEX Yellow

P/T   HMDC · 117

Ideas

= Move away from body
= Ample shapes
= 10 Coats/Capes + 10 Outfits (all based around the Tailored Suit)
∴ 10 models, exit in 10 outfits, re-exit with coats & capes
ie: 30 PIECES

Coats/Capes: Neoprene / Felted Wool (Oversized H'Bone) (Crocheted Rope)

Tailoring: Duchesse Satin / P.O.W. (Birds Eye) / Velvet / Neoprene.
(washed + Raw) (laser-cut)
or 'as is' crumpled.

Reflective Knitwear

Felted/Sheer (Coloured Tights) (a la Toile de Jouy)
– Bold – Simple –

Climbing Shoes

Capes held with climbing accessories / belts made with climbing accessories

RAW Edges (Tensile wire bag protectors?) Part of a Cape!

External seam allowances ranging from narrow to wide

External seam allowances ranging from flat to gathered.

Intarsia shapes (raw edges external)

Isolated volume

Sculptural, contours (for capes, coats) slats

Body fit juxtaposed with volume and voluminous shape

Colour:

All Grey for 10 outfits
colour for tights and knitwear (plus grey)
colour for Capes/Coats.

– Yellow Goretex – seam since pinked
all on outside

¼" seam allowances (Pinked)
Outside edges, raw + pinked
(collection section has perforating panels)
(Yellow goretex, nothing.)

Light neoprene, sewn
normally with inside edges

web tape
inside bag – see
detail?

HMDC · 116

Sketchbooks from the fall-winter 2004-2005 collection

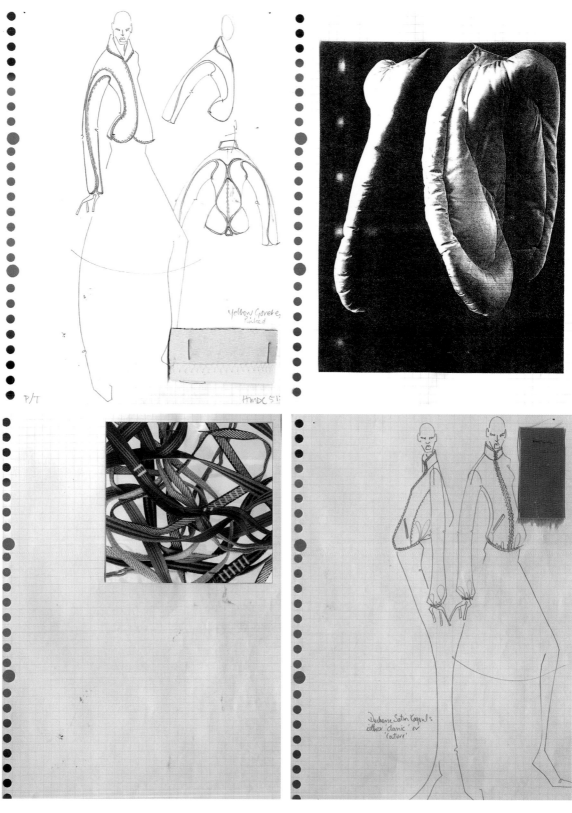

P/T

Yellow Goretex,
Puched

HmDC 51

Duchesse Satin Kagoul's
either 'classic' or
'couture'

Sketchbooks from the fall-winter 2004-2005 collection

Wool or Pertex

HMDC 313

One dream

"Freedom."

'Draped harness'

HMDC 908

Sketchbooks from the fall-winter 2004-2005 collection

Sketchbooks from the fall-winter 2004-2005 collection

Pictures from the fall-winter 2004-2005 collection runway show

Pictures from the fall-winter 2004-2005 collection runway show

Picture from the fall-winter 2008-2009 collection runway show

John Galliano

www.johngalliano.com / www.dior.com

One inspiration

"Daily life; research and experimentation with fabrics; diverse sources to create a completely new look."

Considered as one of the *enfants terribles* of the fashion world, John Galliano was born in Gibraltar in 1960 to a hard-working British family. When he was six, he moved to London. After finishing secondary school in Wilson College, Galliano earned a place in the Central Saint Martins College of Art & Design, where he graduated in 1984 with a collection inspired by the French Revolution entitled "Les Incroyables." The collection received recognition from international press and was purchased by Browns, the most emblematic store in London. Since then, Galliano's career has been nothing short of brilliant.

In 1992, he moved to Paris with his designs of romantic dresses inspired by couture from the fifties and its unsurpassed bias cuts. In 1995, he was appointed as a designer for the Givenchy haute couture and prêt-à-porter collection. Two years later, with the best British designer title under his belt, Galliano was named Christian Dior's creative director.

Each season countless celebrities wear his creations in top cultural and social events. Madonna, Nicole Kidman, Céline Dion, Gwyneth Paltrow and Gwen Stefani are all fans.

Dior amethyst pochette

Pictures of the fall-winter 2008-2009 collection

"Every outfit is thought out to the last detail."

2008 Dior handbags

One dream

"Neverending dreaming."

2008 Dior jewelry

Picture from the fall-winter 2008-2009 collection runway show

Pictures from the fall-winter 2008-2009 collection runway show

Picture from the fall-winter 2008-2009 collection runway show

Sketch from the spring-summer 2007 collection

254 José Miró

José Miró

www.josemiro.com

"Absolutely everything that surrounds me."

Even though José Miró studied design in Barcelona, Paris served as his real fashion school. There, he started his career alongside Thierry Mugler, whom he worked with for three years. At the turn of the new century he returned to Spain. He launched his own collection in 2001, after working as a fashion assistant for Devota & Lomba and manager for the studio and workshop of the ever-original Agatha Ruiz de la Prada.

José's debut at the Pasarela Cibeles 2004 show could not have been better; he presented his Baraka collection and won the L'Oréal Best Young Designer award. In the time that has passed since then, his austere and practical creations, devoid of all excess adornments, have become emblematic of urban fashion. He has received numerous acknowledgements from specialized press. His latest collection has been perfectly and precisely designed with just the right amount of refined sophistication.

In spite of his young age (he was born in 1975), José has worked as a design and fashion lecturer and has shown collections on the best catwalks around the world. In 2005, he became he first Spaniard allowed to present a collection in the Metropolitan during London Fashion Week, and today he is a regular on the red carpet of the British capital.

Final scene of the spring-summer 2007 collection runway show. Photo by Esmeralda Martín

Sketches from the fall-winter 2007-2008 collection

Josep Font

www.josepfont.com

"Impossible to think of only one..."

Josep Font was born in Spain and studied fashion design and patternmaking at the Instituto Internacional Feli. His first success as a professional designer came in 1984 when he won the Air France Competition in Paris, which was followed by an exhibition of his work at the Parisian Fashion and Textile Museum.

Josep presented his first runway collection at the 1989 Cibeles event in Madrid, also taking part in the Contemporary Fashion Fair in Milan and the Piscine Deligny event in Paris that same year. In 1989, he received the Fil d'Argent award, and in 1991 he started his own label, Josep Font. In 1997, the designer began an international business venture, first landing in Tokyo where he presented his spring-summer collection, and a short time later in Paris where he began a professional collaboration with Galeries Lafayette and subsequently sold from his Laboratoire des Créatures (designer laboratory) collection. His next step was to open his own store in the Parisian rue Sourdière.

Among the prizes Josep has won during his short, but successful, career are the bottle of Esprit du Siècle by Moët & Chandon, which acknowledged him as a notable designer of the new millennium, and the *Elle* magazine 's 2001 Style Award. He currently presents his collections at the Paris prêt-à-porter and haute couture shows.

Picture of the spring-summer 2008 campaign

Picture of the fall-winter 2007-2008 campaign

"Any piece with that special something."

One dream

"Whatever comes after haute couture will be very welcome."

Pictures from the haute couture spring-summer 2008 collection runway show

Sketches from the fall-winter 2006-2007 collection

Juan Antonio López

www.juanantoniolopez.com

One inspiration

"The forties."

In spring 2002, Juan Antonio López presented his first collection staying loyal to the handcrafted production process that he witnessed in his father's factory in Alicante. His father's process had instilled in him that the art of making a shoe is expressing one's know-how, both regarding the technique and the aesthetics. This is why he calls himself a shoemaker before a designer. His collections reflect these premises.

The images that bring to mind the classic shoe with a low-cut front, thin tall heel are endless. Atemporal designs, a reduced array of materials and an almost architectural manufacturing process define his shoes. The passion with which he thinks, the sincerity with which he works and the dedication of the entire manufacturing process result in what he considers "the essence" of a female shoe. Juan has dreamed about shoes like these since he was born.

Juan's collections are inspired by different time periods. Classic style elements and fits coexist with the modern details that personalize each piece. Mono or bicolor models, high heels or flat—his objective is always to extol the values that characterize femininity. Today, Juan has stores in Madrid and Barcelona and is one of the favorite shoe designers of the most prestigious editors of international fashion magazines such as *Vogue*, *Marie Claire* and *Glamour*.

Sketches from the fall-winter 2006-2007 collection

Sketches from the fall-winter 2006-2007 collection

One garment

"Gloves."

C.I.F B-62558184 - tel (34) 93 452 66 90/fax (34) 93 452 66 93
informacion@juanantoniolópez.com

Sketches from the fall-winter 2006-2007 collection

One dream

"My illusion, my project, my people united."

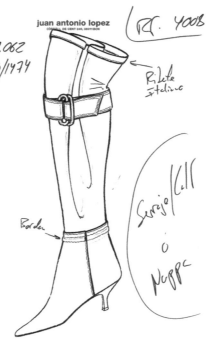

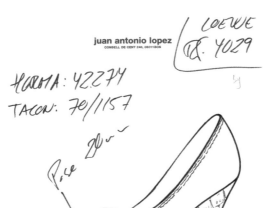

Sketches from the fall-winter 2006-2007 collection

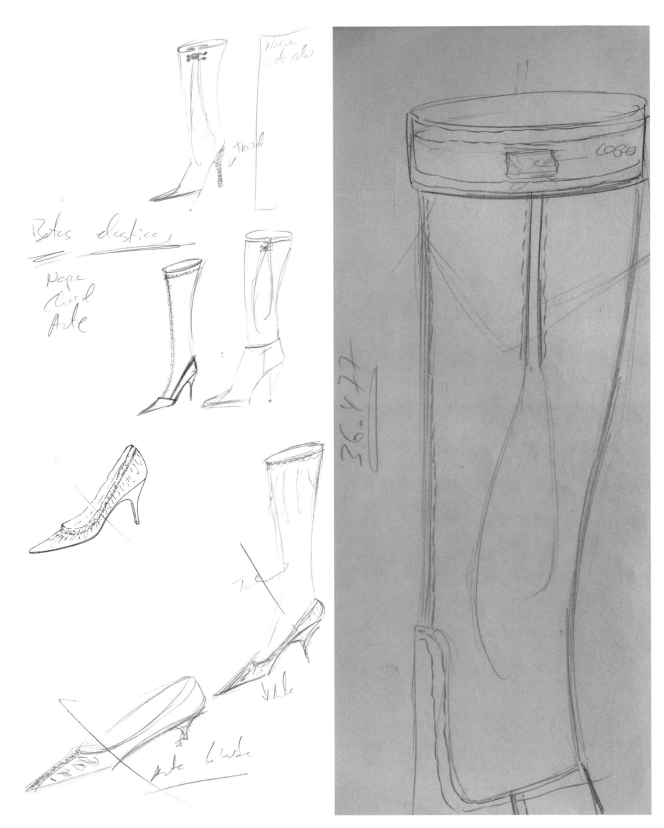

Sketches from the fall-winter 2006-2007 collection

Sketches from the fall-winter 2008-2009 collection

Juun.J

www.juunj.com

"Neoclassicism."

Juun.J was born in Seoul, South Korea, in 1967, and felt the attraction of the fashion world from a young age. After graduating from ESMOD Seoul, he joined the design team at the Chiffon label, where he produced his first pieces as a professional designer. He later went to work for Club Monaco until an offer from Nix for the position of creative director paved the way for his definitive rise.

After acquiring the necessary experience, Juun.J went solo in 1999 and designed a men's collection, Lone Costume, under his own label. Between 2000 and 2006, the young designer took part in the Seoul Fashion Week runway shows. Since 2007, he has been presenting his collections at the Paris Men's Prêt-à-Porter shows. Juun.J's style of design is based on his personal ideas and inspiration. He has a great preference for combining themes, different silhouettes and anything to do with technological innovation, yet his methods are based on traditional tailoring.

A faithful follower of the most cutting-edge art movements, Juun.J has collaborated on projects with the Japanese artist Nuts and with Simon Henwood from Britain. His pieces are featured on the pages of men's fashion magazines, such as *Vogue Uomo* and *GQ*.

Pictures from the fall-winter 2008-2009 collection

Sketches from the fall-winter 2008-2009 collection

One garment

"A trench coat."

Picture from the spring-summer 2008 collection runway show

Sketches from the fall-winter 2008-2009 collection

One dream

"To make timeless items."

Picture from the spring-summer 2008 collection runway show

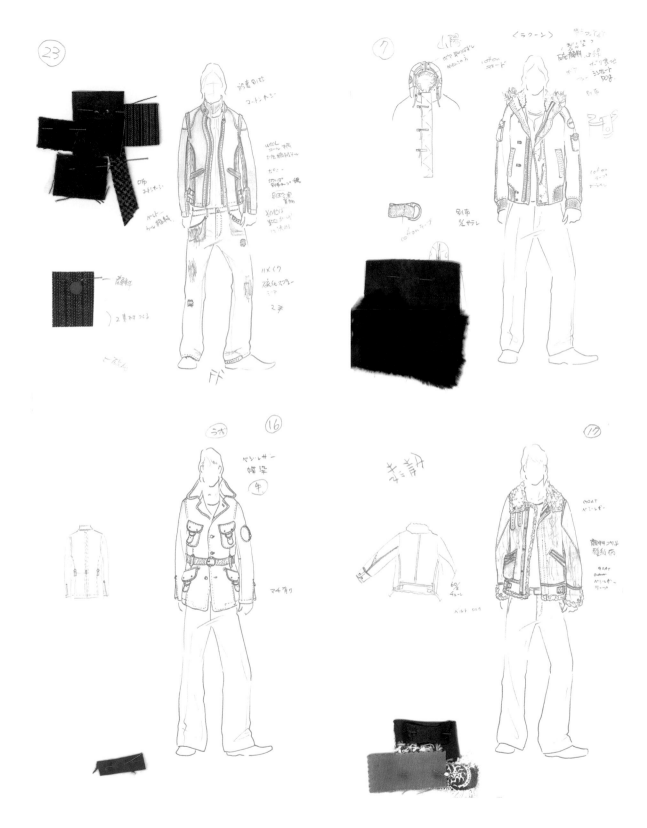

Sketches from the fall-winter 2008-2009 collection

Kiminori
Morishita

www.totemfashion.com

One inspiration

"Antoine de Saint-Exupéry."

Born in the Japanese city of Hiroshima, Kiminori Morishita's career in fashion began in 1986 as assistant to Kazutaka Katoh, founder of Tête Homme, with whom he trained in the areas of sewing, design and patternmaking. After his experience as creative director of Tête Homme Garnier in 1994 and at Tête Homme in 1998, Kiminori finally created his own label, in 2002.

Kiminori presented his first collection on the runway of Tokyo Fashion Week in 2003. He moved his shows to Paris in 2005. His work is based on experimentation with fabrics. He acknowledges the constant inspiration he receives from military uniforms and traveling, and shows his preference for defined silhouettes and precision-cutting in his designs.

Kiminori's clothes are elegant, luxurious, and aristocratic, which is evident in his combining jackets with vests and bow ties, although his line also includes more casual pieces such as jumpsuits and overalls. Besides working on his own label, Kiminori has collaborated on the development of other brands like Halb. His pieces are sold in select establishments such as Dantone in Milan, L'Eclaireur in Paris, Maxfield in Los Angeles and Harvey Nichols in London.

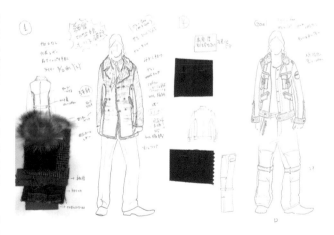

Sketches from the fall-winter 2008-2009 collection

Sketches from the fall-winter 2008-2009 collection

One garment

"A vest."

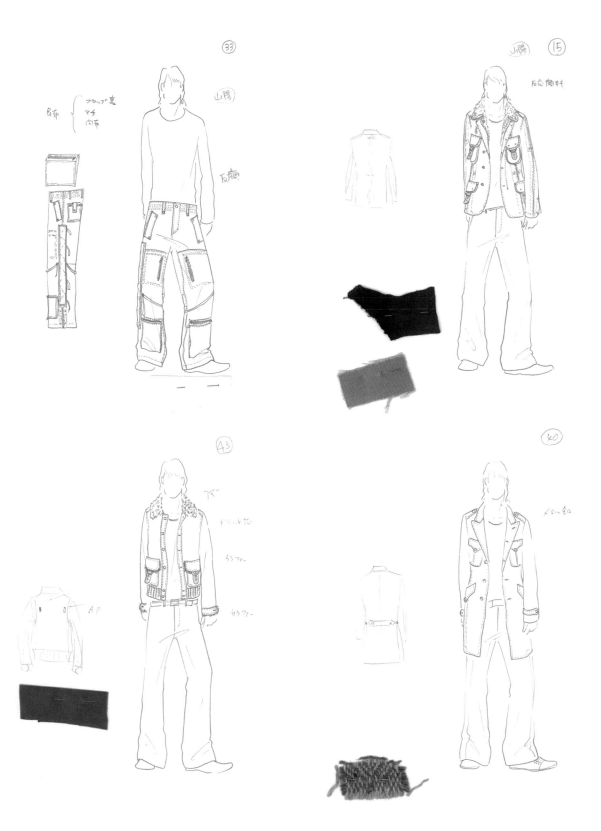

Sketches from the fall-winter 2008-2009 collection

ラクーン
一重.

ライナー
ニッキス袖なし

エルク.

メダリオン
ブートオイル

Sketch from the fall-winter 2008-2009 collection

One dream

"A journey."

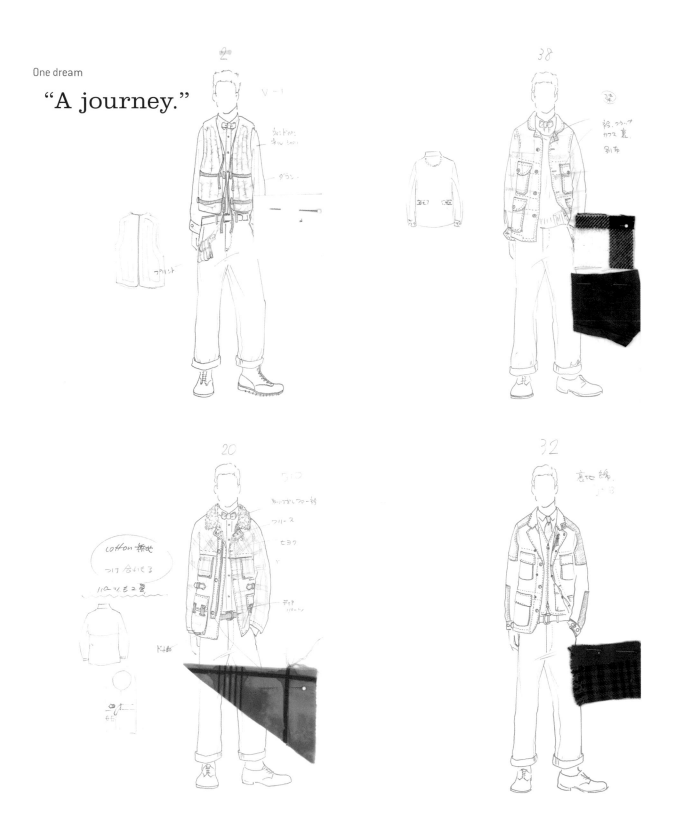

Sketches from the fall-winter 2008-2009 collection

Pictures from the fall-winter 2008-2009 collection runway show

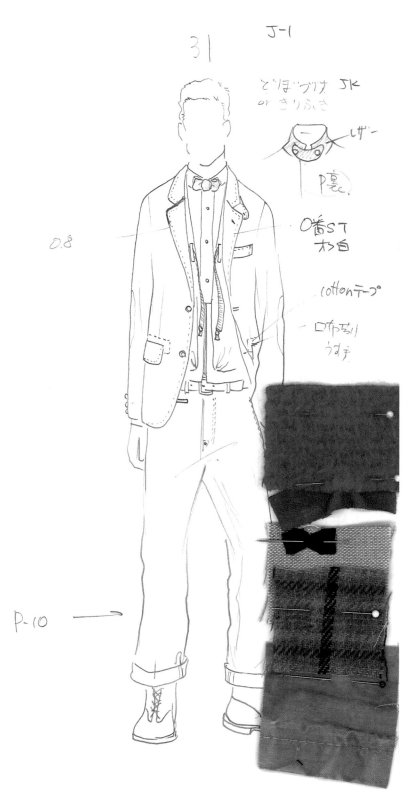

31   J-1

どうぼづけ JK
の きりふさ

げー

P 裏.

0番ST
わ白

cotton テープ

ロかちょい
うすチ

0.8

P-10 ———→

Sketch from the fall-winter 2008-2009 collection

284 Kiminori Morishita

Picture from the fall-winter 2008-2009 runway show

Sketches from the fall-winter 2008-2009 collection

Kina
Fernández

www.kinafernandez.es

One inspiration

"Paris. I lived there from the age of eighteen to twenty-six. I continue to visit it every now and again, and as soon as I step onto the streets of Paris, I am filled with emotion. When I retire, I would like to have a second home in Paris."

Galician designer Kina Fernández showed interest in fashion from an early age. When she was twenty, she moved to Paris to learn all that she needed to know to set up a label in 1995.

Designer, business woman and mother, Kina is a perfectionist and has excelled in the world of design for her careful cuts and selection of top quality fabrics. Currently she is the creative director of her company's three labels, Kina Fernández, Klub, and Kina Difusión, and she presents her collections during Madrid Fashion Week. The key to her designs is to create elegance and empower femininity as a whole. The simplicity of her creations and her desire to reach a large public base are the foundations of all her collections. Tailored suits, three-quarter length coats made from typically male fabrics, along with elegant dresses make up collections free from ostentatious accessories.

Kina Fernández designs have different points of sale in Spain and can be found all over Europe and Latin America in multi-brand spaces. Kina has been awarded by different institutions and the media both for her career as a designer and her career as a business woman.

Sketches from the fall-winter 2007-2008 (left) and fall-winter 2008-2009 collections (right)

One garment

"The well-tailored black male blazer that even after all these years, still remains modern, classy and an essential for all wardrobes."

Sketches from the fall-winter 2007-2008 collection

Pictures from the fall-winter 2008-2009 collection runway show

"I think to a certain extent, I have achieved my dreams. Now my dreams are my grandchildren."

Sketches from the spring-summer 2005 collection

Picture from the fall-winter 2008-2009 collection runway show

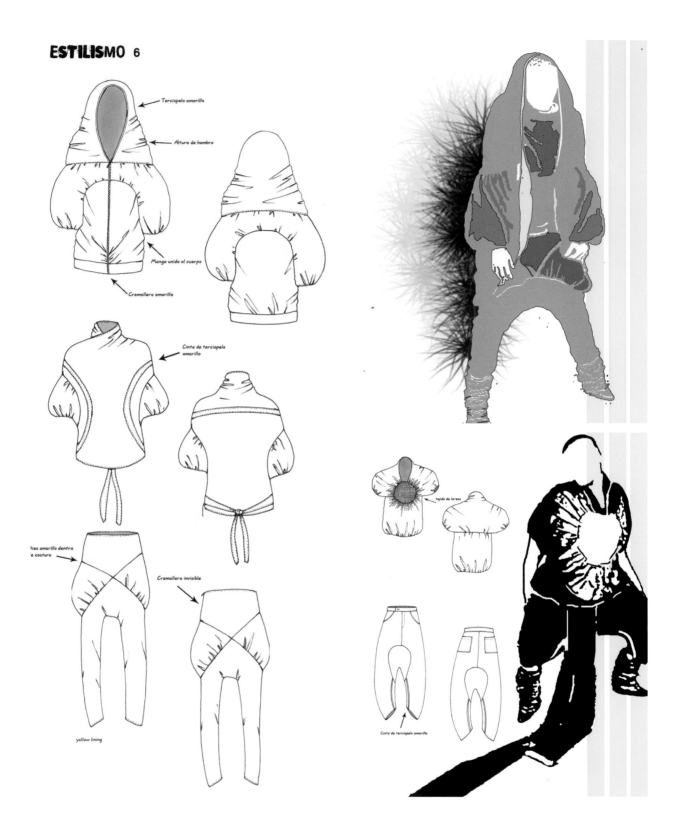

Terciopelo amarillo

Altura de hombro

Manga unida al cuerpo

Cremallera amarilla

Cinta de terciopelo amarilla

hies amarillo dentro e costura

Cremallera invisible

yellow lining

tejido de lursas

Cinta de terciopelo amarilla

Images from the Street Life fall-winter 2007-2008 collection

Krizia
Robustella

www.kriziarobustella.com

One inspiration

"The streets."

Born in Amsterdam in 1984, Krizia Robustella belongs to a new generation of talented young designers trained in Barcelona. A student at the Felicidad Duce Design and Fashion College, she has worked in the design department of Konrad Muhr. Since 2006, she has had run her own atelier where she designs her collections and manages her own label.

Sport clothes are the base of Krizia's style. She blends comfort with luxury using fabrics banned until now in prêt-à-porter. She also enjoys using track suits as both experimental and basic pieces. The foundations of the Krizia Robustella's look are dynamic colors and materials from the eighties and the nineties.

Recycling old pieces and revisiting earlier ideas of taste are an essential part of the collections she calls "sport deluxe fashion": sweatshirts lengthened to become minidresses, shoulder pads sharing the stage with tracksuit pants and black and gold featured on pieces adorned with sequins and sparkles.

Despite her youth, Krizia's creations are featured on the pages of some of the biggest names in cutting-edge fashion publications, such as *Pig*, *Neo2*, *View of the Times*, and *Kult*.

Images from the Street Life fall-winter 2007-2008 collection

One garment

"The tracksuit."

Images from the Street Life fall-winter 2007-2008 collection

Las prendas están diseñadas a partir de chandals de los años 90'. Los cortes de patchwork no se pueden definir hasta una vez realizada la prenda.

Goma elástica interior

Cinta de punto cosida sobre cuerpo

Vivo entre costura

Abertura con cremallera

Images from the Street Life fall-winter 2007-2008 collection

One dream

"Krizia Robustella
on the red carpet."

Images from the Street Life fall-winter 2007-2008 collection

Image from Street Life fall-winter 2007-2008 collection

Lunch print for the spring-summer 2008 collection

La Casita de Wendy

www.lacasitadewendy.com

One inspiration

"Friends, food, art."

Inés Aguilar and Iván Martínez, both from Madrid, are the two de-signers behind La Casita de Wendy, one of most popular European labels, which is reflected in the fact that many celebrities from the world of television, cinema and music have all worn their designs. The most well-known example is the singer and actress Björk, who has chosen their designs for cover shoots for prestigious maga-zines, such as *The Wire*, *Les Inrockuptibles* and *Vogue*, and for ap-pearances on the BBC.

Their clothes are characterized by the use of a select palette of colors, simple lines and contrasting patterns that they design themselves. Their passions and inspirations are music, fairytales and magic, and their main tool is their imagination. Their projects have been very varied: specific orders to design collections such as a Powerpuff Girls collection alongside Cartoon Network that was exclusively created for EKS or their participation in the Absolut's 2004 campaign.

La Casita de Wendy clothing is distributed from its showrooms in Paris and Madrid, and is sold internationally in stores such as Barneys in New York, Cocktail in Hong Kong, Matsuya y Baycrews in Tokyo, Liborius in Iceland, and Henrik Vibskov in Denmark. The company also has more than seventy points of sale in Spain.

Flores Colores print for the spring-summer 2008 collection

Print and sketches from the spring-summer 2008 collection

Comida Rosa print for the spring-summer 2008 collection

One garment

"Anything with patchwork."

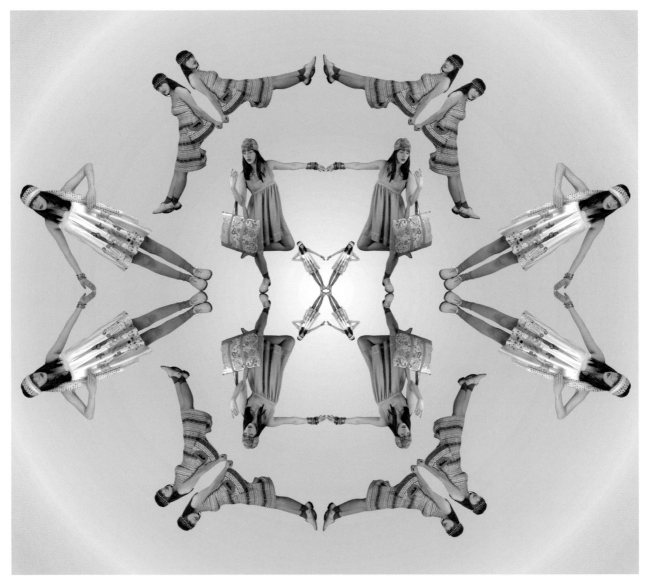

Picture from the spring-summer 2008 collection. Photos by Ramiroe

Picture from the spring-summer 2008 collection. Photos by Ramiroe

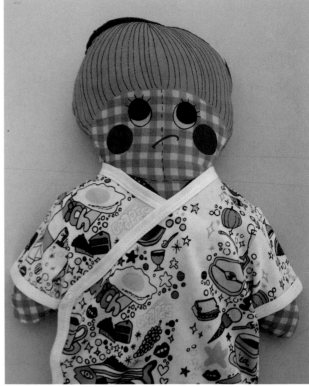
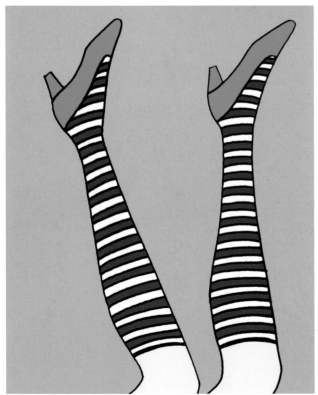

Pictures from the spring-summer 2004 and 2006 collections. Photos by Ramiroe

One dream

"To be invisible."

Print from the spring-summer 2008 collection

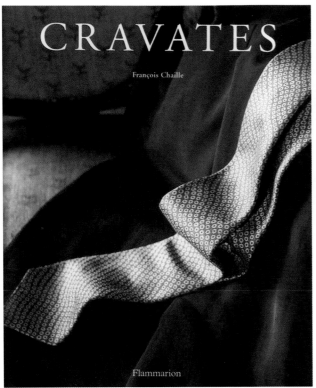

CRAVATES

François Chaille

Flammarion

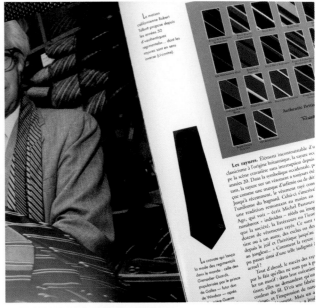

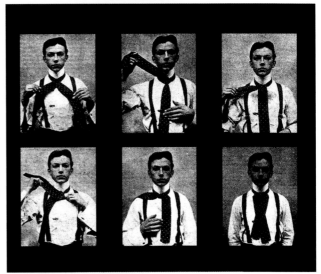

Fall-winter 2008-2009 collection

Laura B
Collection
Particulière

www.laurab.info

One inspiration

"The twenties."

Laura Bortolami was born in Rome in 1962 from an Italian father and Dutch-Indonesian mother. After studying translation and interpreting in Geneva, her life took a U-turn at the hands of Caterina Salvador, then Armani's primary assistant. She accepted a position in the sales department at Giorgio Armani, and then went on to work for other top-tier designers such as Gianni Versace, Anna Molinari, and Dolce & Gabbana.

Laura moved to the south of France in the early nineties, and it was here that she combined her passion for antique jewelry with her desire to develop cutting-edge techniques. Taking metal mesh as her signature material, Laura creates unique jewelry by combining the metal meh with other materials such as silver, gemstones, leather and crocodile skin. This led to the creation of the jewelry line Laura B Collection Particulière, which features a number of exclusively distributed collections.

She moved her firm to Barcelona in 1995, where, in 2003, she decided to create her first men's collection, which jewelry, belts and neckties. Among her latest collaborations, one she did in 2009 with Jean Paul Gaultier for his prêt-à-porter and haute couture collections. Laura B pieces can be found in the most select retailers in the world, such as Dieci Corso Como in Milan, Barneys in both Tokyo and New York, L'Eclaireur in Paris, Browns and Liberty in London and Maxfield in Los Angeles.

Inspirational objects for the spring-summer 2008 collection

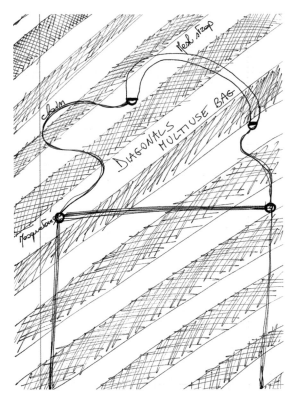

One garment

"Shoes."

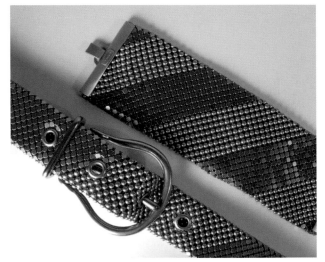

Diagonals fall-winter 2008-2009 collection

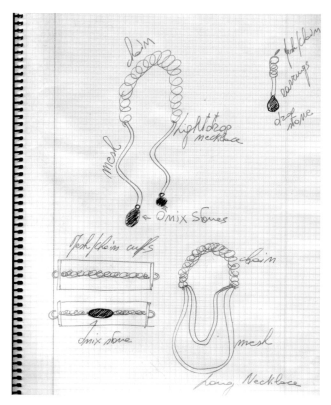

One dream

"Laura B boutiques in the most important cities in the world."

Mesh & Chain fall-winter 2008-2009 collection

Image from the Photobook 1 fall-winter 2008-2009 collection

Lorena Rodríguez

www.lorenarodriguez.es

One inspiration

"Architecture."

Born in Ourense, Spain, in 1979, and influenced by her family's artistic background, Lorena Rodríguez studied fashion design, patternmaking and scaling. She also broadened her education with studies in window-dressing and wardrobe techniques. After a brief experience working with designer Cristóbal Vidal, she began a fruitful collaboration with Roberto Verino.

Lorena's diverse professional experience allows her to develop a unique look characterized by the use of architectural metaphors and the absence of color and ornamental details. The poetry found in her work lies in her subtle mastery of proportion and the exquisite elegance of the cut of her clothing, which is always finished with great precision as a reaction to overelaborate styles and the overwhelming visual saturation existing today. Her latest collection (spring-summer 2010) featured black and white, showing her inclination for clean lines to dress an essentially urban woman.

Despite her short career, Lorena Rodríguez has received three important acknowledgments: the 2006 Tesoira Prize, awarded by the government of the Galician region, the 2007 Mostra do Encaixe International Prize and the 2007 Murcia Joven National Prize. Her collections are shown in the El Ego section of the Cibeles Madrid Fashion Week.

Images from the Photobook 1 fall-winter 2008-2009 collection

One garment

"A dress."

Images from the Photobook 1 fall-winter 2008-2009 collection

Image from the Photobook 1 fall-winter 2008-2009 collection

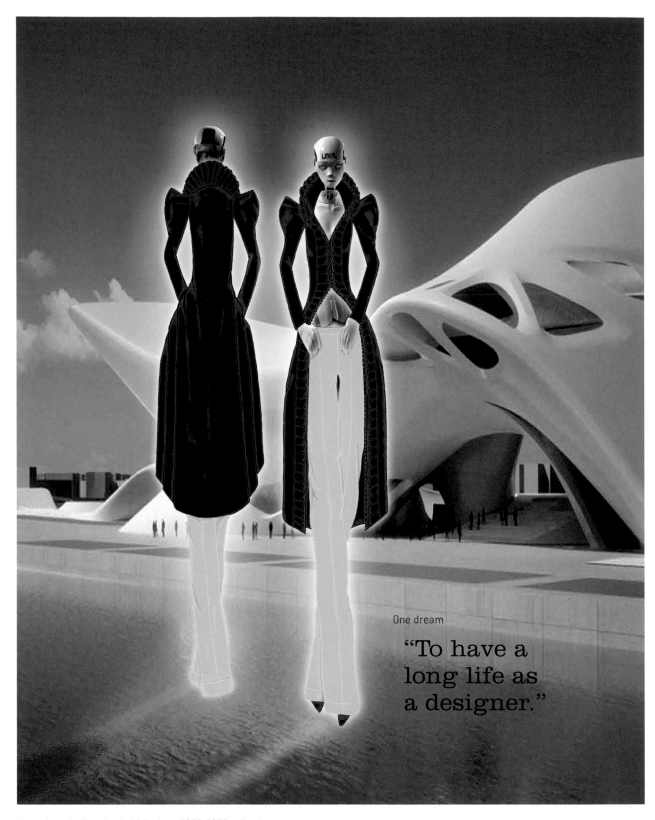

One dream

"To have a long life as a designer."

Image from the Photobook 1 fall-winter 2008-2009 collection

Image from the Photobook 1 fall-winter 2008-2009 collection

Sketch from the spring-summer 2009 collection

Louis
Féraud

www.feraud.com

One inspiration

"Mediterranean spirit of life."

Born in Arles, France, in 1921, Louis Féraud created his design house in Cannes in 1950. Among his clientele were actresses who attended the city's famous Film Festival, such as Brigitte Bardot. Later he became a theatre costume designer, and in 1955 he moved to Paris where he opened a prêt-à-porter workshop.

As an amateur painter, Louis drew inspiration from the art of other cultures, especially Latin-American culture, and he expresses this inspiration in all his collections. In 1958, he took his first steps in haute couture and soon became a member of the designers club made up of Christian Dior, Cristóbal Balenciaga, Jeanne Lanvin and Hubert de Givenchy, and his fame extended to Europe, the USA and Japan. Louis Féraud designs show a certain level of sensitivity especially in the use of color and since the sixties some of his garments have become fashion classics.

Jean Pierre Marty is now the creative director of Louis Féraud. Just as his predecessor, his Mediterranean origins have marked his creative career. From a family of artists—his mother was a muse of Dalí—, Jean Pierre worked for Yves Saint Laurent and Kenzo before his appointment as creative director of Guy Laroche. Since he joined Féraud in 2005 he has managed to maintain the aesthetic principles of the company in his female, male, accessory and jewelry collections. The company has more than fifty stores around the world.

Sketches from the spring-summer 2009 collection

One garment

"All that represents a vision of a very female Parisian style, a sort of a draft of a new concept of contemporary couture."

Sketches from the spring-summer 2009 collection

Sketch from the spring-summer 2009 collection

Sketches from the spring-summer 2009 collection

Picture from the fall-winter 2008-2009 collection

One dream

"Designing, designing, designing…"

Picture from the fall-winter 2008-2009 collection

Pictures from the fall-winter 2008-2009 collection

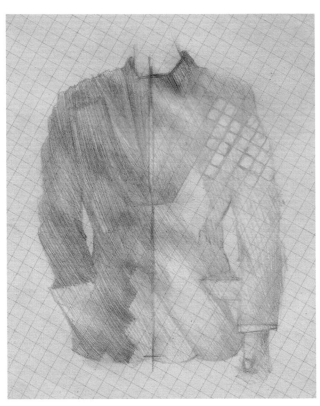
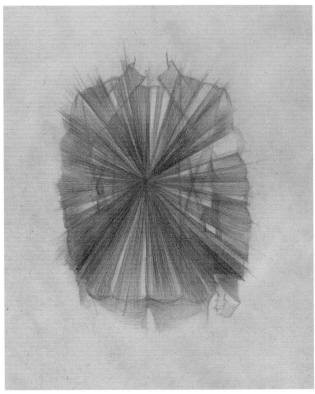
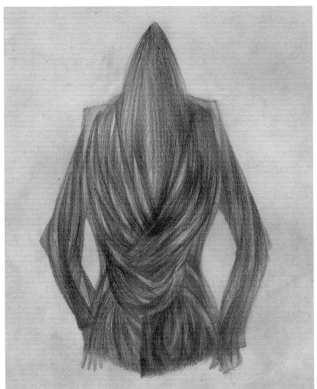
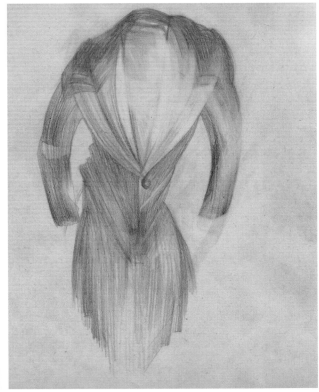

2008 sketches

Mammifères de Luxe

www.mammiferesdeluxe.com

"A puff of air."

Korean-born Kyu-in Chae studied at the National Superior School of Decorative Arts and in Chambre Syndicale de la Haute Couture in Paris. Between 2001 and 2006, he worked as a designer in John Galliano's creative team for his two labels: John Galliano and Christian Dior Couture. A few years later, in 2007, he launched the first male collection of the newly-created brand Mammifères de Luxe in Paris.

From the beginning, this young designer's collections have emphasized technical details without being ostentatious. Kyu-in has developed new archetypes in the field of fashion, like the pocket with silhouette. For him, a pocket is not just a simple detail. He uses it for both functional and ornamental purposes, which is why an entire collection is based on an element that is normally relegated to secondary roles. His specialty are extravagantly designed jackets that are carefully made with details that although they cannot be seen, characterize each piece.

Today Mammifères de Luxe is one of the fetish labels of fashion editors around the world. Its collections are presented during Paris Fashion Week, and its garments fill the pages of fashion magazines such as *Vogue*, *Elle* and *Jalouse*.

2008 sketches

One garment

"A jacket."

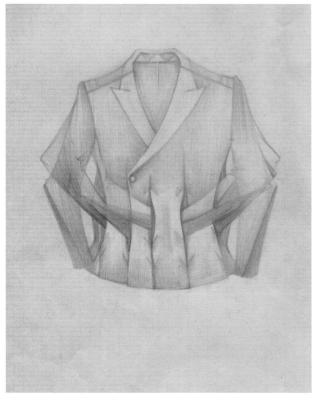

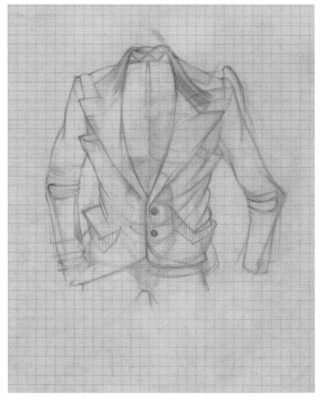

2008 sketches

Pictures from the spring-summer 2008 collection

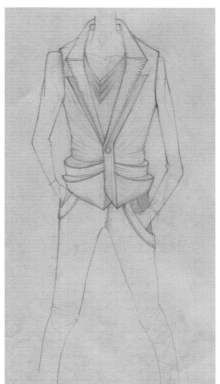

One dream

"A balance."

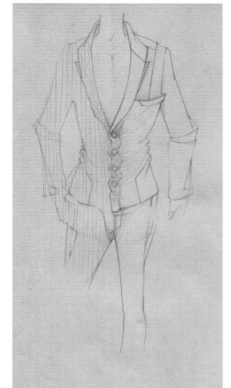

2008 sketches

2008 sketch

reversible!!

bies + plisado

muelle

Sketch from the fall-winter 2008-2009 collection

Martin
Lamothe

www.martinlamothe.es

One inspiration

"Music."

Elena Martín, attracted by both fashion and architecture, graduated from the Barcelona Art and Fashion School and received a First Class degree from the University of Southampton in the UK. As a twenty-year-old, she was the youngest student admitted to the prestigious Central Saint Martins College of Art and Design where she earned a master's degree, in which she developed her passion for structure and graphics. Her first student collection appeared in magazines such as *Self Service* and *International Textiles*.

When she finished her studies, Elena worked for Marcus Constable and RL, and as a stylist alongside Mr. Jones for celebrities such as Kylie Minogue and Howie B. She also participated in theatre plays and experimental movies in London's East End. When she went back to Barcelona, she took over the design management for the denim collection of Antonio Miró, Miró Jeans. In 2006 after completing four seasons in the company and giving seminars at fashion schools and art universities, Elena established her own label, Martin Lamothe, based on the creation of an original universe of graphics and forms.

In 2007, Martin Lamothe launched a prêt-à-porter unisex line that was greatly accepted by the male public. The international label currently can be found in Australia, Japan, Korea, USA and, of course, Europe.

Flyer for the Symbols spring-summer 2007 collection

One garment

"A cloak."

Sketches from the fall-winter 2008-2009 collection

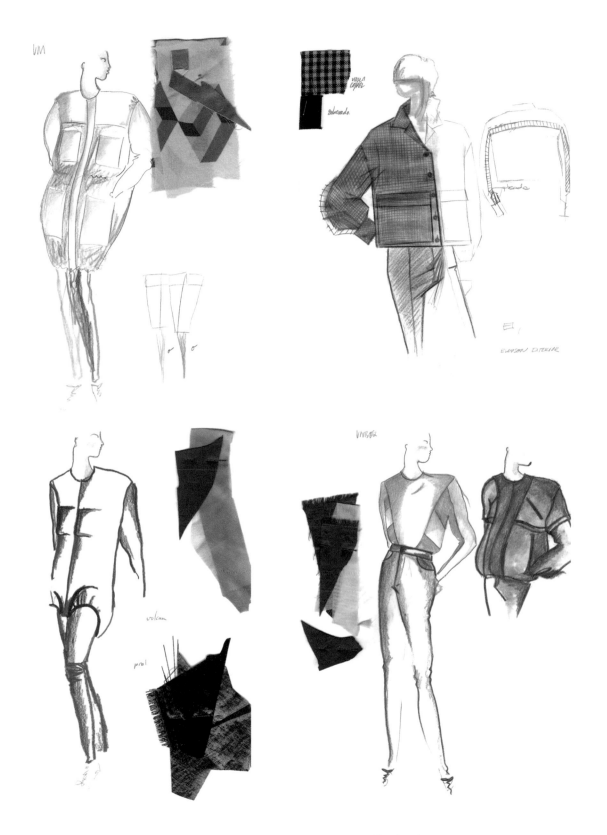

Sketches from the fall-winter 2008-2009 collection

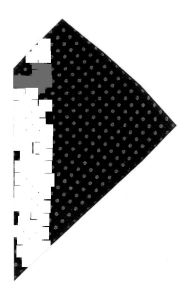

One dream

"An endless multicolor t-shirt."

Sketch from the fall-winter 2008-2009 collection

Pictures from the Sandokan II fall-winter 2008-2009 collection runway show

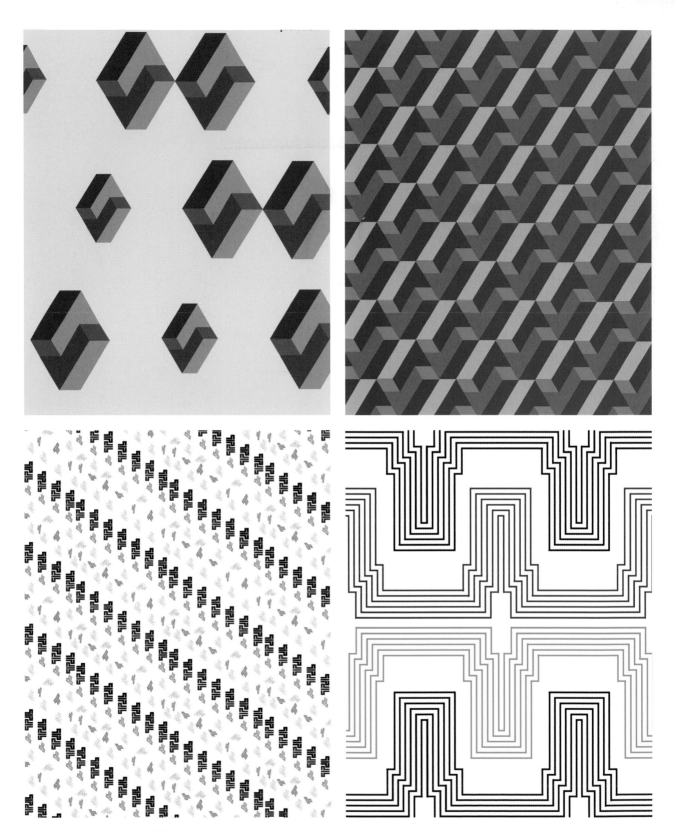

Prints from the spring-summer 2008 collection

Sketch from the spring-summer 2008 collection

Sketches from the fall-winter 2008-2009 collection

Masatomo

www.masatomo-paris.com

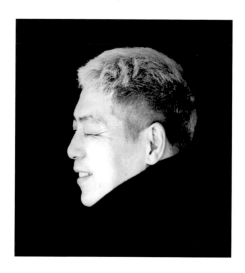

One inspiration

"My own desire; I make clothes I want to wear myself."

The tradition of good tailoring and perfect finishing is the base from which Masatomo collections have been created for twenty years. Designer Rynshu Hashimoto started the Ma-Ji firm in 1985, which then became Masatomo in 1992. He opened his first Paris store in Place des Vosges in 1996, and a year later was designing suits for celebrities such as Mick Jagger.

Masatomo collections rely on a the magic formula: the cleanest lines of traditional tailoring mixed with a touch of elegance. While the line's jackets and pants are strongly masculine in their cut, all Masatomo pieces are made from traditionally feminine fabrics. According to the designer, "feminine elements add the right amount of luxury to the male silhouette." Rynshu's inspiration comes from typical Japanese elements, while the application of different features such as Swarovski crystal and gold are features of his style.

Masatomo has been presenting its collections in Paris since 1992, with this city being the location for one of the label's boutiques (the other is in Tokyo). Today, Masatomo is a leading label for a number of Hollywood stars of the likes of Robert de Niro, Al Pacino, Jack Nicholson, Jennifer Lopez and Whoopi Goldberg.

Final scene of the fall-winter 2008-2009 collection runway show

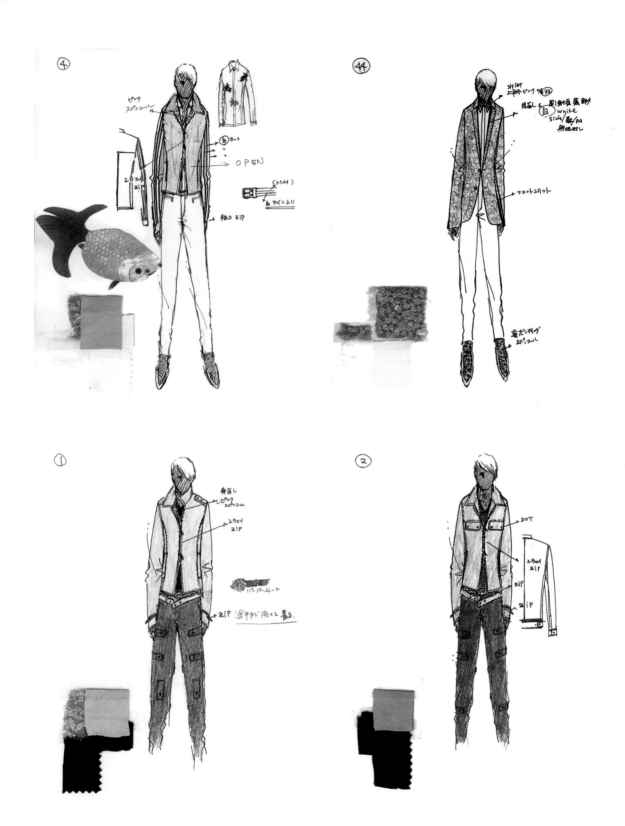

Sketches from the fall-winter 2008-2009 collection

One garment

"A black leather blouson."

Picture of a look from the fall-winter 2008-2009 collection runway show

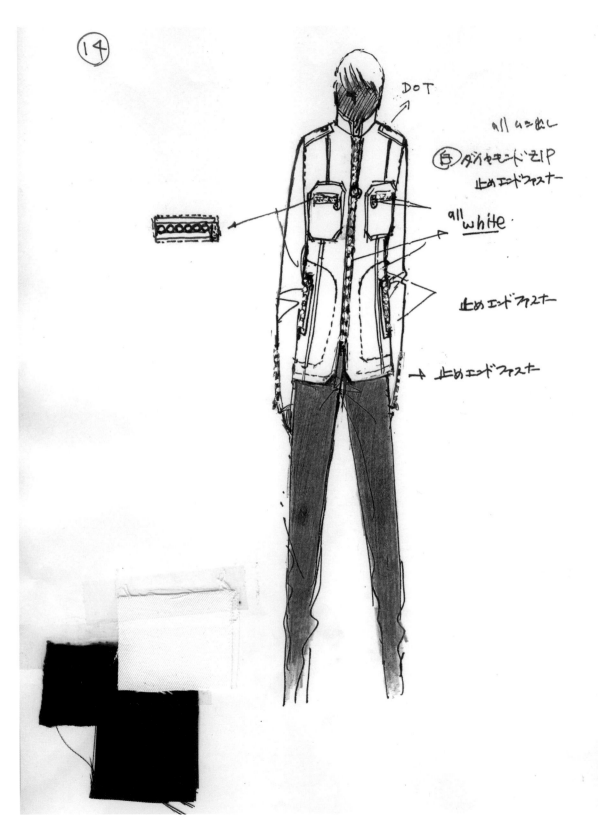

DOT

all ゴニ出し

⑥ ダイヤモンド ZIP
止め エンドファスナー

all white

止め エンドファスナー

止め エンドファスナー

Sketch from the fall-winter 2008-2009 collection

342 Masatomo

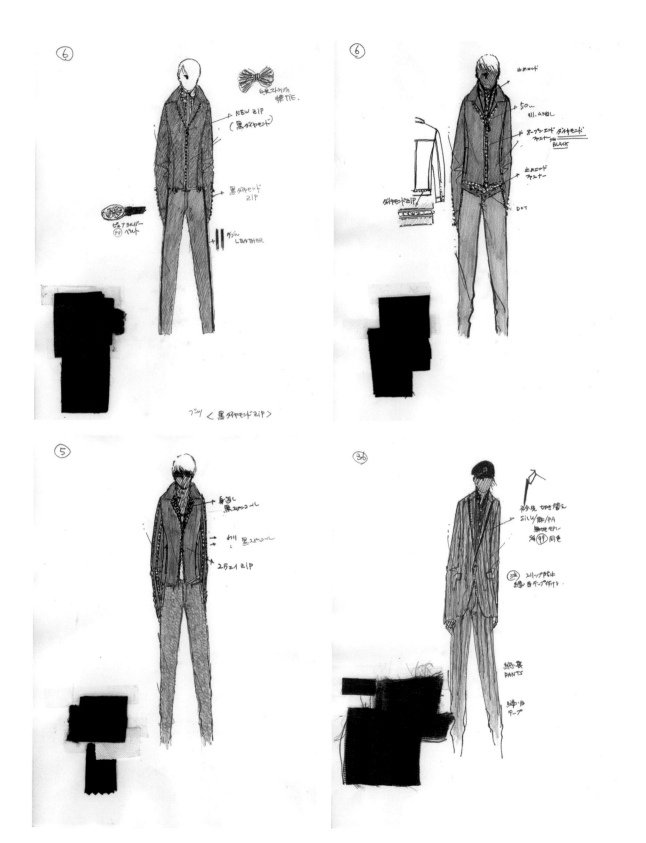

Sketches from the fall-winter 2008-2009 collection

One dream

"As I made it come true in Japan this year, I can say my next dream is to make movies in Hollywood! Making costumes, but also writing, directing and producing too…"

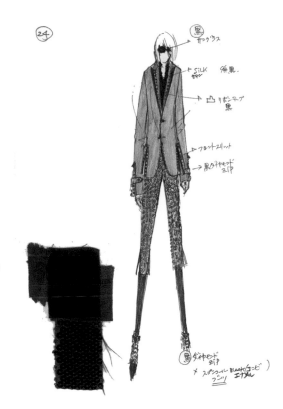

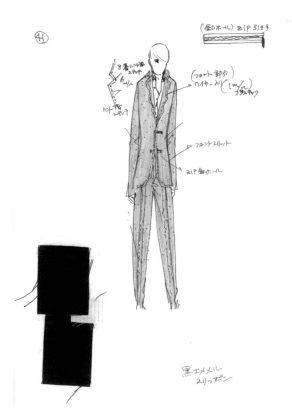

Sketches from the fall-winter 2008-2009 collection

エポーレット

PATなし

→裏地（背底）
BLACK に
金魚インクジェットプリント
（オレンジ赤5匹）

Sketch from the fall-winter 2008-2009 collection

Sketch from the fall-winter 2008-2009 collection

Picture of a look from the fall-winter 2008-2009 collection runway show

OSCARE

Sketch from the spring-summer 2008 collection

Modernist

www.modernistonline.com

One inspiration

"Contrast. We don't look at fashion in a historical sense and we hardly look at existing garments."

Modernist collections are based on contrast. Andrew Jones and Abdul Koroma, the duo behind the label, come from very different backgrounds although their ideas and personal taste come together to create well thought-out collections with modern lines.

Born in 1975 in Northumberland, a part of the North East of England, Andrew Jones was an extremely intuitive boy and from an early age, he showed a great interest in design. Andrew studied fashion at the University of Kingston and later moved to Italy to work with the prestigious company Max Mara. Abdul Koroma was born in Sierra Leone in 1977. He moved to London in the nineties to study architecture. However, at the last moment he decided to study fashion, enrolling in the same course as Andrew.

Some years later, they met again working for Max Mara. In 2005, they decided to join forces to form a kind of creative matrimony with impressive aesthetic symbiosis. Abdul's leanings towards architecture have had a great influence on their collections' pure lines, attention to detail, clarity of cut, proportion and lack of unnecessary details, hence the prevalence of austere dresses they've created with romantic touches that feature lace or organdy details. Their collections are on sale in Harvey Nichols in London.

Sketches from the spring-summer 2008 collection

"Pieces that suggest different things and inhabit a sartorial grey area."

Pictures from the fall-winter 2008-2009 collection runway show

FRINGE

Sketches from the fall-winter 2008-2009 collection

"To have our own store/atelier where we could fully express our concept and ideas that go beyond just fashion design to include other disciplines like graphic design, music, illustration, photography and writing."

Sketches from the fall-winter 2008-2009 collection

solid

shade.
[maybe organza?]

or graphic
black + ECRU?

-washed duchess?

Sketches from the fall-winter 2008-2009 collection

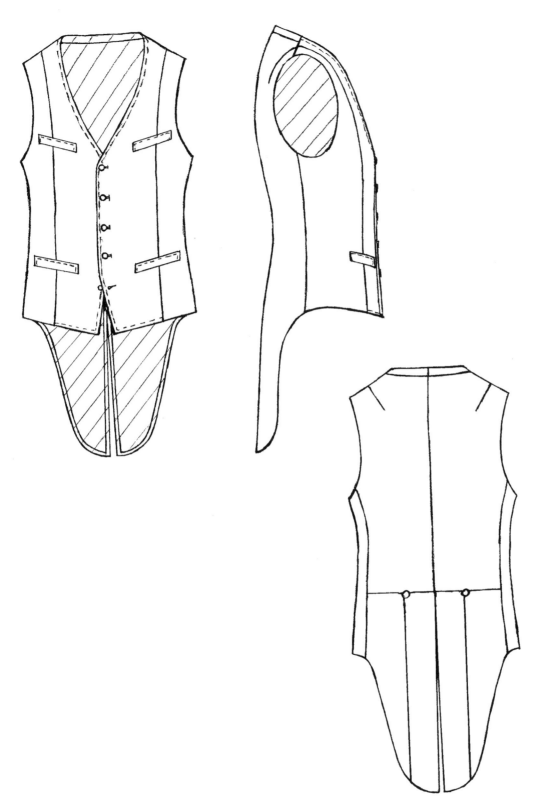

Sketches from the fall-winter 2007-2008 menswear collection

Neil Barrett

www.neilbarrett.com

One inspiration

"Anything and everything."

Born in Devonshire, England, in 1965, Neil Barrett's passion for design stems from his grandparents who were tailors by profession and passed on their love for cuts and refined clothing to Neil. After graduating from Central Saint Martins in 1986 and earning a master's degree at the Royal College of Art, Neil was appointed as senior designer at Gucci in Florence where his work contributed to the creative and financial revitalization of the label.

The success Neil achieved for the Italian firm opened the doors for him to another prestigious brand, Prada, for which he created his first collection of menswear. In 1998, he designed a collection under his own name, which was successful, and his pieces were sold in hundreds of stores around the world. A year later, Neil created the White label for Prada and in 2000 he presented his first female collection. His next step was a deal with Puma to create a line of athletic footwear.

Neil's collections have always been characterized by a restrained use of detail and perfect cuts supported by a thorough understanding of the production of textiles. Most of his garments are designed using neutral and discreet colors. His fans include Orlando Bloom, Kirsten Dunst, Jake Gyllenhaal, Chris Martin, Ewan McGregor, Brad Pitt, Mark Ruffalo, and Naomi Watts.

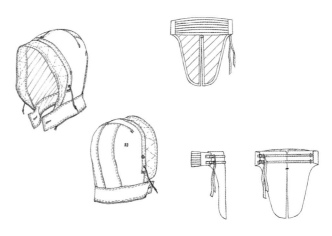

Sketches from the fall-winter 2007-2008 menswear collection

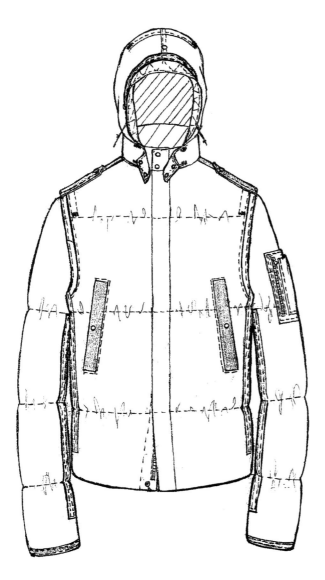

One garment

"Any…"

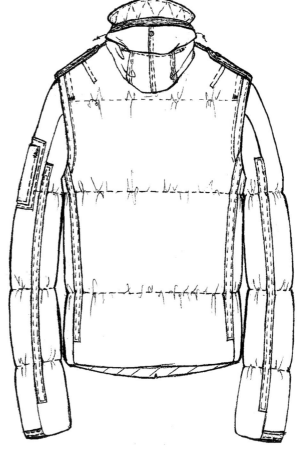

Sketches from the fall-winter 2007-2008 menswear collection

Sketches from the fall-winter 2007-2008 menswear collection

Sketches from the fall-winter 2007-2008 menswear collection

One dream

"To keep enjoying the work that I do."

Sketches from the fall-winter 2008-2009 collection

Phi

www.phicollection.com

"Urban women."

Although it is a new label in the world of fashion, Phi is a benchmark in fashion, especially in the North American market. Andreas Melbostad is the creative director of this brand, and his collections are inspired by the New York urban lifestyle.

Born and bred in Norway, Andreas wanted to be a fashion designer from a young age. He studied at the Norwegian College of Art and Design in Oslo and then he earned a master's degree in fashion design at the Royal College of Art in London. Andreas started off his career working with Nicole Farhi in the English capital before moving to Paris to work with Alber Elbaz for Guy Laroche and for Yves Saint Laurent's Rive Gauche. He also worked with Nathalie Gervais at Nina Ricci before being headhunted by Calvin Klein and moving to New York.

In October 2003, he joined Phi after working for Donna Karan as the head of design for the female fashion collection. His designs are a true reflection of the current needs of the urban woman: comfortable garments with architectural cuts, perfectly constructed silhouettes, sober colors and minimal and functional details. Phi distributes its designs all over the world through points of sale in the USA, France, Canada, Italy, Australia, Korea, Germany, the Ukraine and Russia.

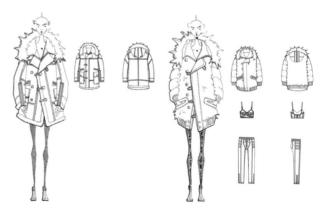

Sketches from the fall-winter 2008-2009 collection

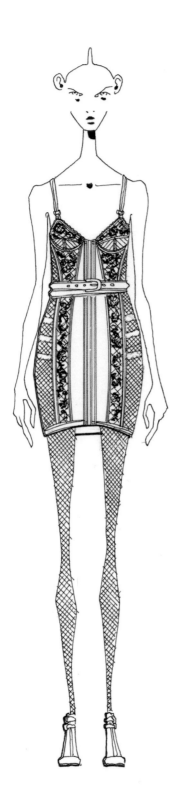

Sketches from the fall-winter 2008-2009 collection

One garment

"Any with a perfect cut."

One dream

"Design."

Sketches from the fall-winter 2008-2009 collection

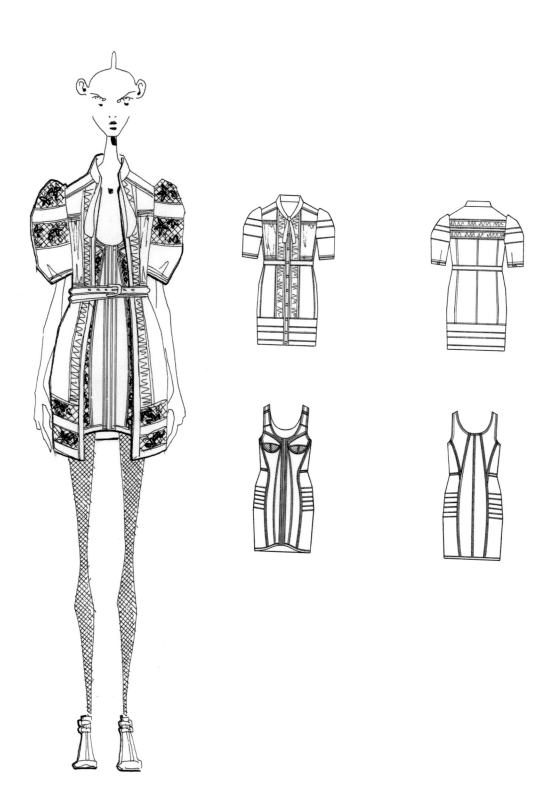

Sketches from the fall-winter 2008-2009 collection

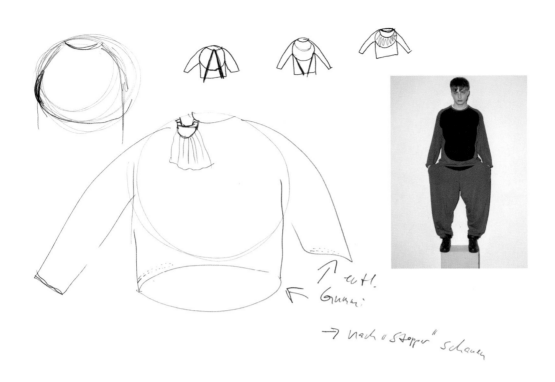

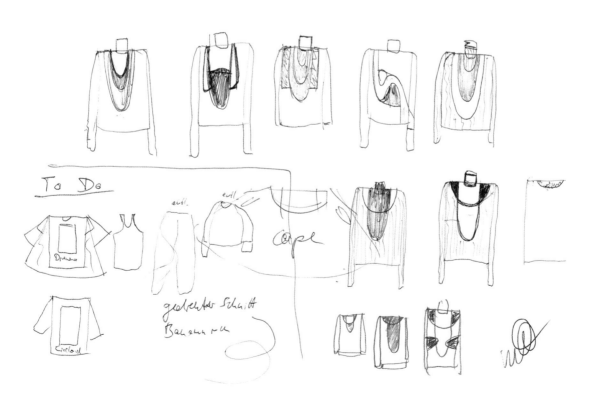

Sketches from the fall-winter 2006-2007 menswear collection

Postweiler
Hauber

www.postweilerhauber.com

"People that live in their own world, even if it may seem strange to others."

Postweiler Hauber is a fashion label formed by German designers Eva Postweiler and Raphael Hauber. Both designers studied design at HFG Pforzheim in Germany and graduated with distinctions in 2003. In August of that same year, they set up their own label. Their collections are a clothing for both men and women.

In March 2004, the first Postweiler Hauber collection, titled Because the Middle is Inside, was presented in Paris. In most Postweiler Hauber collections, it is usual to find colors such as bright white, silver, neon yellow, pinks, grays and materials such as viscose, chintz and plastic mixed with cotton. However, their spring-summer 2006 collection, The Night in Your Mind, surprised critics for its use of an unusual chromatic range that brought together gold and turquoise with materials such as lurex and lycra. This collection, a clear tribute to David Bowie and T. Rex glam, has become one of the most emblematic of the creative duo.

Today, Postweiler Hauber fashion shows are held in Paris and Berlin. Its clothes are in Japan, Munich, Amsterdam and Barcelona. Both designers have individually participated in the exhibition "Found for you" in the Quartier Museum in Vienna, directed by Wendy & Jim. Postweiler Hauber garments often grace the pages of *i-D*, *Dazed & Confused Japan*, *Vman*, *Arena Homme*, *Neo2*, *Squint Homme*, *Sleek* and *032c*.

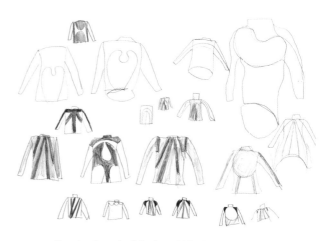

Sketches from the fall-winter 2006-2007 menswear collection

Sketches from the fall-winter 2006-2007 menswear collection

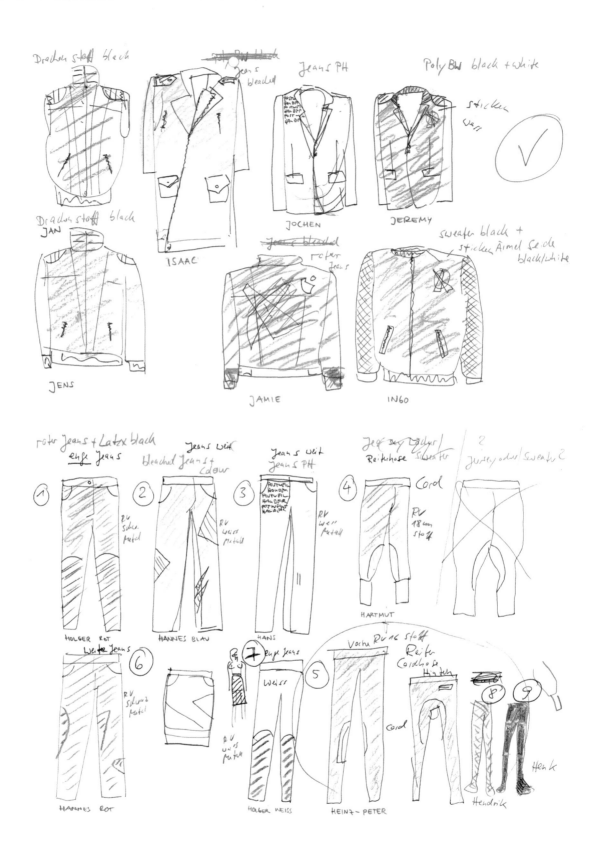

Sketches from the fall-winter 2006-2007 menswear collection

"The circle shirt from the fall-winter 2008-2009 collection. Simple, but effective."

 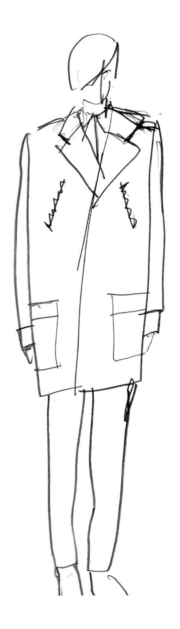

Sketches from the fall-winter 2006-2007 menswear collection

"Love, money and the world in the Postweiler Hauber craze."

Sketches from the fall-winter 2006-2007 menswear collection

Sketch from the fall-winter 2007-2008 collection

Rui Leonardes

www.ruileonardes.com

"Pollution."

Considered one of the most controversial designers of the moment, London-based Rui Leonardes reenvisioned male fashion. Born in Azores, Portugal, he studied male and female fashion design at the Gerrit Rietveld Academie in Amsterdam. After graduating, he moved to Paris where he worked for Nina Ricci Homme and for Jose Levy where he was supervised by Hedi Slimane, creative director of the label. Later, he decided to expand his knowledge and moved to London to study footwear design at the Royal College of Art.

In 2005, Rui launched his own collection, and since then he has become one of the most sought-after British designers. The madness of his creative energy is based on an intellectual approach to design: shapes and subversive constructions that he creates in advance of the final design. His visionary proposal for men to wear heels marks a before and after in contemporary male fashion.

Rui has participated in three Manolo Blahnik Awards in Italy, in the exhibition "Future of Menswear" and at the Victoria & Albert Museum in London, and he helped to design the wardrobe for artists such as the Scissor Sisters. His collections are presented at London Fashion Week.

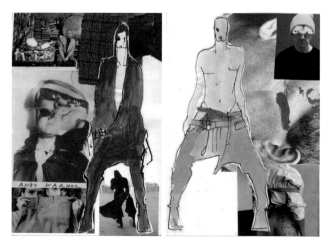

Images and sketches from the fall-winter 2007-2008 collection

Images and sketches from the fall-winter 2007-2008 collection

Images and sketches from the fall-winter 2007-2008 collection

"Mickey Mouse's jacket."

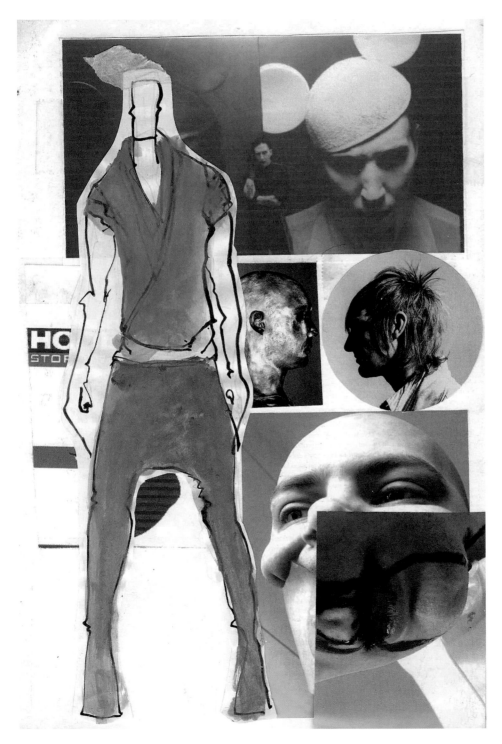

Images and sketches from the fall-winter 2007-2008 collection

One dream

"To open an animal rescue center."

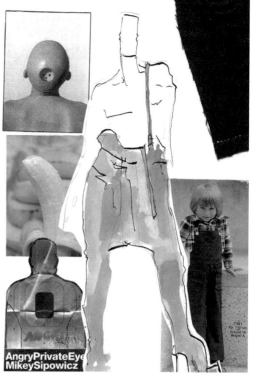

Images and sketches from the fall-winter 2007-2008 collection

Sketches from the fall-winter 2008-2009 collection

Sharon Wauchob

www.sharonwauchob.com

One inspiration

"Inspiration for me is the morning, each winter morning early outside in the country before the day has started."

Born in Northern Ireland in 1971, Sharon Wauchob graduated with a special mention in fashion design from Central Saint Martins College of Art & Design in London. Her talent was soon noticed by industry critics and professionals, and she moved to Paris to become design assistant to Koji Tatsuno. Shortly afterwards, she joined the design team at luxury goods firm Louis Vuitton before launching her own label, S. Wauchob, in 1998, and presenting her first collection in October of the same year.

Wauchob's designs are divided into her main line and Collection K, a knitwear collection that is gradually finding a niche among the most well-known labels in the industry. The S. Wauchob style brings together strength and femininity with risqué color combinations and contrasts. Known for her innovative designs and quality work, Sharon constantly strives to make a difference while keeping her originality.

The S. Wauchob label is currently available around the world in 100 stores in 23 countries, including the L'Eclaireur stores in Paris and Tokyo, Lane Crawford in Hong Kong and Henri Bendel in New York. Her plans for the future include developing new product lines, such as accessories and perfumes.

Sketches from the spring-summer 2008 collection

Sketches from the spring-summer 2008 collection

One garment

"Impossible to choose. The last idea is always the best, the one that gives a surprise."

Sketches from the fall-winter 2008-2009 collection

One dream

"Dreams for me are in the evening, special evenings relaxing in Ireland on the beach."

Sketches from the fall-winter 2008-2009 collection

Pictures from the fall-winter 2008-2009 collection runway show

Pictures from the fall-winter 2008-2009 collection and spring-summer 2008 collection runway shows

Picture from the spring-summer 2008 collection runway show

Sketches from the spring-summer 2008 collection

Sinpatron

www.sinpatron.com

One inspiration

"Day-to-day experiences with people around me and fabrics."

A self-taught designer from Bilbao, Spain, Alberto Etxebarrieta made a successful debut in 2004 in the third edition of the Modorrra Fashion Show. His collection, made up of controversial punk garments featured the skirt as a unisex garment.

Since then, Alberto's designs have been based on a search for extremes, the baroque and the military, and feature enormous money belts amongst other surprising accessories. He feels passionate about XXL jackets, tracksuits, wide silhouettes, daring volumes and bold colors both for men and women; his favorites are yellow, black, and green.

After participating in a number of editions of the Modorrra Fashion Show with avant-garde collections, such as one inspired by the decline of Berlin in the thirties, Etxebarrieta won the 2007 Bizkaia Council award for Best Male Collection and received honors at the FIB Mustang Fashion Weekend.

Alberto has worked with an endless list of artists, such as video-creator Raquel Meyers and musician Rubeck, with whom he developed a project showed at the latest edition of the San Sebastián International Film Festival. He has also dressed artists and musicians such as Yogurinha Borova, Félix Daniel, Lourdes Madow and Begoña Muñoz.

Sketches from the spring-summer 2008 collection

Sketches from the spring-summer 2008 collection

"Scottish tartan."

Sketch from the spring-summer 2008 collection

One dream

"To be able to
enjoy what I
love the most."

Sketch from the spring-summer 2008 collection

Sketch from the spring-summer 2008 collection

Moodboard from the spring-summer 2008 collection

Steve J
& Yoni P

www.steveyonistudio.com

"We look towards African farming to explore the use of handcraft techniques to manipulate their fabrics, producing sculptural and three-dimensional forms."

Steve Jung and Yoni Pai form part of a new wave of renowned designers. They met in Korea and both studied design at Central Saint Martins College of Art & Design in London. Steve specialized in female fashion and Yoni in menswear. While they were studying, they decided to create their own label.

This duo's designs are a summary of references coming from different cultures—from Tibetan to African tribes—, but always applying British tailoring principles. Their collections have a level of sensitivity originating from daily realities, always with a preference for exquisite fabrics and daring cuts.

They have a brazen, direct and fun style. As well as designing their own collections, Steve and Yoni work for other popular labels such as Topshop. Their undeniable talent has granted them acknowledgment in the industry, such as the 2006 Best Masculine Designer Award from Central Saint Martins and the 2007 Samsung Fashion & Design Fund.

Steve J & Yoni P collections are presented during London Fashion Week. The label's garments, which can be found in London, California, Russia and Korea, fill the pages of the trendiest magazines, such as *Vogue*, *Flux*, *Wallpaper*, *Androgyny*, *Luxure* and *Nylon*.

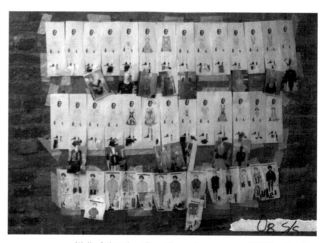

Wall of sketches from the spring-summer 2008 collection

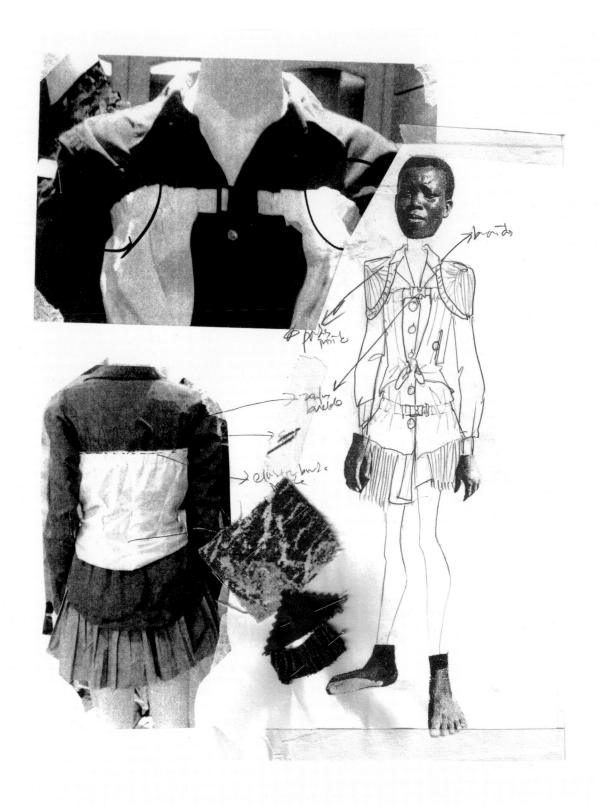

Moodboard from the spring-summer 2008 collection

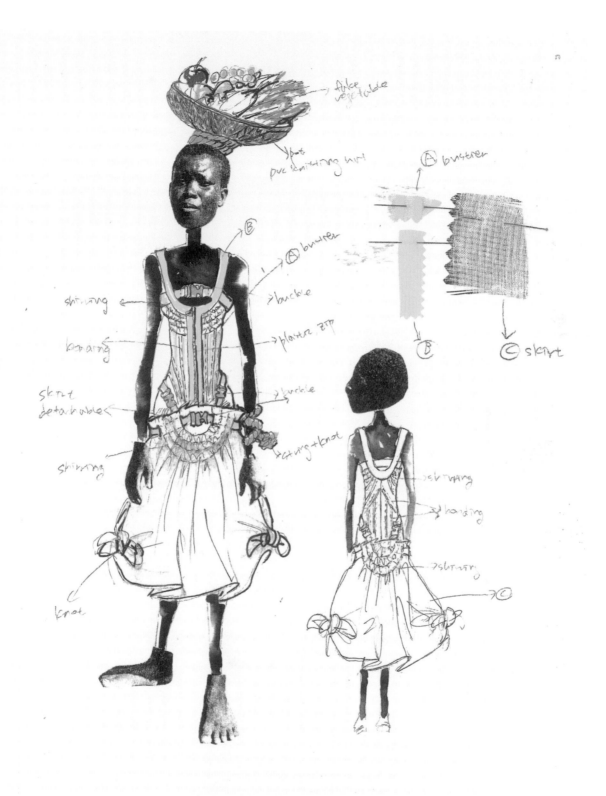

Moodboard from the spring-summer 2008 collection

Moodboard from the spring-summer 2008 collection

One garment

"Any with handicraft elements with twisted piping running along the hem of garments and braiding decorates the bodice as well as outline bust-lines."

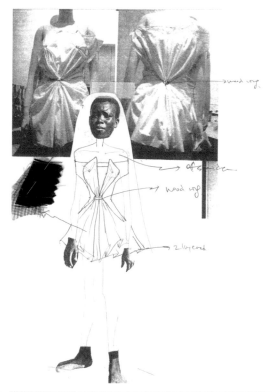

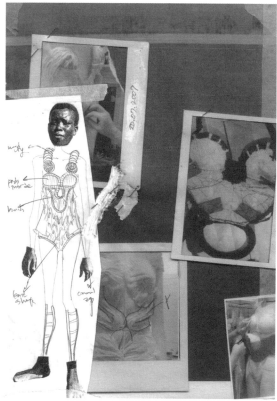

Moodboards from the spring-summer 2008 collection

"We want to build
up our label's image
through the innovative
catwalk show and
open the Steve J &
Yoni P concept store in
London."

Moodboard from the spring-summer 2008 collection

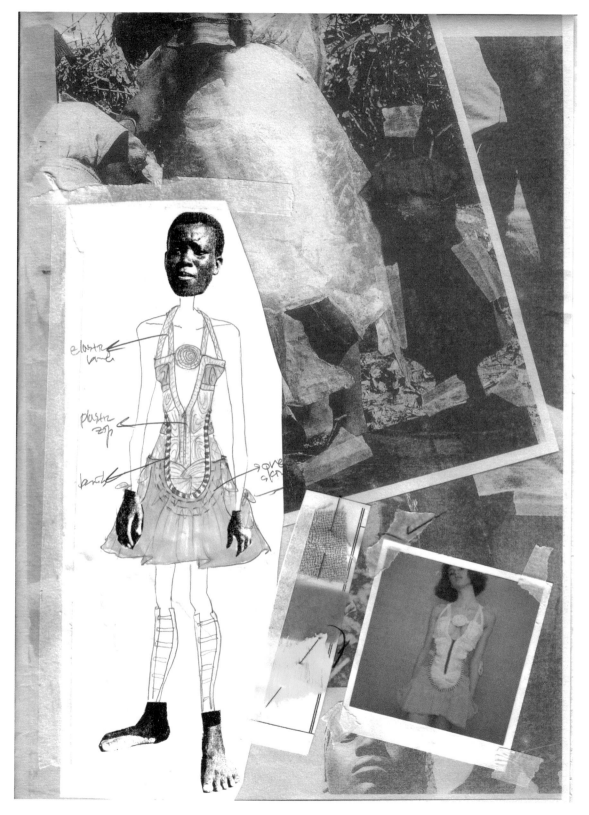

Moodboard from the spring-summer 2008 collection

Picture from the fall-winter 2008-2009 collection

Temperley
London

www.temperleylondon.com

One inspiration

"Life, beauty and the infinite creative possibilities that we have."

British designer Alice Temperley was born in 1975. After studying design from Central Saint Martins, she earned a master's degree from the Royal College of Art. In 2000, she created the company Temperley London with her husband, Lars von Bennigsen. The brand grew gradually until it diversified into a tailored collection, knitwear, a Black Label limited edition collection and a bridal collection.

Alice has shown a special skill in advanced techniques of textile prints. This has granted her acknowledgments such as the Central Saint Martins Award for Innovation, the Print Designer of the Year 1999, the Best Designer Award from the British magazine *Glamour*, the award for Best Young Designer of the Year from the British edition of *Elle* and the Walpole award. She has also been considered one of the most influential business women in the UK.

The Temperley London brand has just four stores, one each in London, New York, Los Angeles and Dubai, but its designs can be found in boutiques as prestigious as Selfridges, Harrods, Harvey Nichols in the UK, Neiman Marcus and Saks Fifth Avenue in the USA, Harvey Nichols and Boutique 1 in the Middle East, 10 Corso Como in Milan, and Gum and Tsum in Russia, as well as on net-a-porter.com, neimanmarcus.com, and on the label's own website.

Moodboard (2008)

Pictures from the fall-winter 2008-2009 collection

One garment

"Clothes."

Fitting of the Mimosa Petal jacket from the fall-winter 2009-2010 collection

Sketches and photos from the fall-winter 2008-2009 collection

Designing the Lotus Intarsia Petal dress from the fall-winter 2009-2010 collection (top) and a sketchbook from 2008 (below)

Picture from the fall-winter 2008-2009 collection

One dream

"To be happy
and enjoy the
health of loved
ones."

Pictures from the fall-winter 2008-2009 collection

Picture from the fall-winter 2008-2009 collection

Sketch from the spring-summer 2009 collection

Tillmann Lauterbach

www.tillmannlauterbach.com

One inspiration

"Daily life and magic."

Born in Bonn, Germany, in 1977 and raised in Ibiza, Spain, Tillmann Lauterbach studied in Germany and Switzerland. When he was 18, he decided to move to Barcelona, where he carried out a training course at Deutsche Bank. While working there, he developed several artistic projects, worked as a model for magazines such as *Marie Claire*, *GQ* and *Uomo* and created advertising campaigns for Paul Smith, Levi's and Lacoste, among other brands.

In 2000, Tillmann decided to make changes in his life and he followed the call of fashion to Paris. He enrolled in the famous Esmod School of Design where he earned a degree in in design and patternmaking, and obtained his first award as a designer. After his graduation, he was hired by the Plien Sud label.

In 2005, Tillmann presented his first collections in Paris and Vienna, which included designs both for men and women. White and petrol blue are some of his favorite colors. He enjoys a minimalistic approach to his designs, so the pureness of his cuts plays with asymmetries. He also has a clear passion for the use of fabrics like wool or pure cotton and for maxi accessories. His garments have been presented at Paris, Frankfurt, Barcelona and Basel Fashion Weeks.

Moodboard (2007)

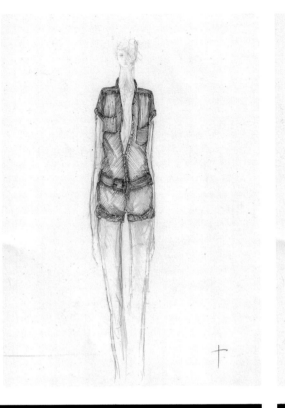

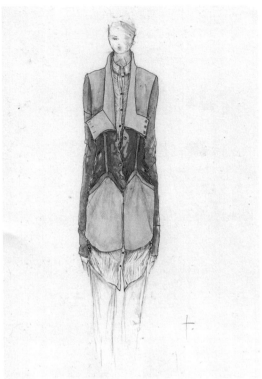

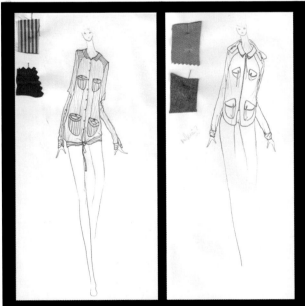

Sketches from the spring-summer 2007 collection

One garment

"Each piece for a special moment."

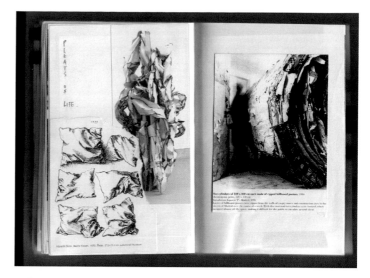

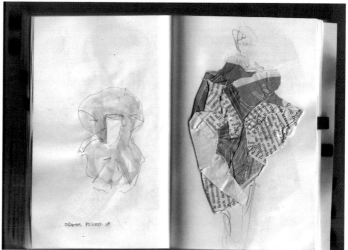

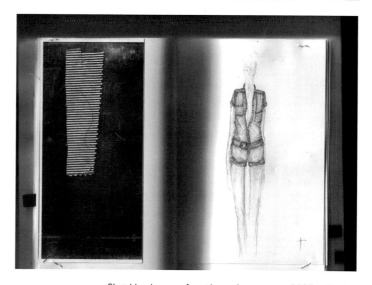

Sketchbook pages from the spring-summer 2007 collection

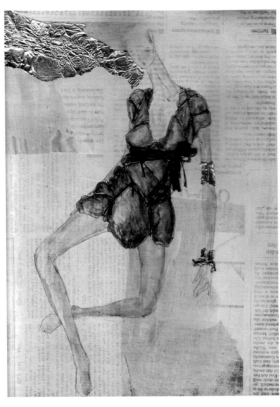

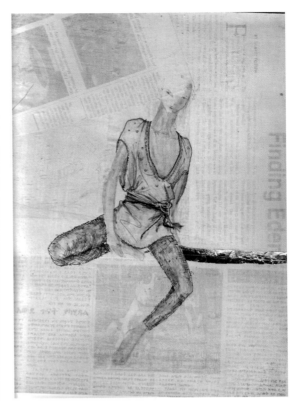

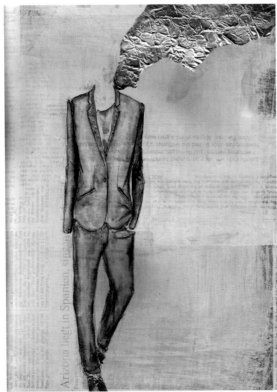

Sketches from the spring-summer 2009 collection

One dream

"Not to be sleepy."

Picture from the spring-summer 2009 collection

Happy Stuff print from the spring-summer 2007 collection

Tsumori
Chisato

www.tsumorichisato.com

One inspiration

"My spirituality and sixth sense."

Born in Saitama, Japan, Tsumori Chisato studied fashion at the famous Tokyo Bunka School. In 1977, she began to work with Issey Miyake as head of design of Issey Sports, which was later renamed IS Chisato Tsumori Design. In 1990, she then created her own label, Tsumori Chisato, and held her first fashion show in Tokyo.

In 1999, Tsumori opened her company's first store on rue Barbeta in the Parisian district of Marais. The famous architect Christian Biecher took charge of the boutique's design. In 2002, Tsumori was named "best designer" by the Japanese newspaper *Mainichi*. The use of intricate details and luxurious material stands out in her designs. Like many of her compatriots, she shies away from rigid cuts and provides a delicate fluidity to her designs.

She launched her first menswear fashion collection in 2003. Since then, she has presented her collections during the Prêt-à-Porter Paris week. Her shows are crowded with editors from the main international fashion magazines. Today, Tsumori distributes her designs all over the world. There are more than forty points of sale for the Tsumori Chisato label around Asia, including three flagship stores in Tokyo and one in Kobe, and its popularity continues to grow in Europe and the USA.

Sketch from the spring-summer 2007 collection

Sketches from the spring-summer 2007 collection

One garment

"A dress that makes you young and beautiful!"

One dream

"To be able to communicate with everything and everyone in the world."

Pictures from the spring-summer 2007 collection runway show

Picture from the spring-summer 2007 collection runway show

Picture from the fall-winter 2006-2007 collection

Txell Miras

www.txellmiras.eu

One inspiration

"Anything interesting or stimulating."

After graduating from the University of Barcelona, designer Txell Miras started out on her career by winning the Insideouting competition held by the Domus Academy in Milan. As her prize, she received a scholarship for a master's degree in fashion design. She was a finalist in the 2002 Onward Grand Prix international competition in Tokyo, and a year later she was named Italy's most promising young designer by the Italian Fashion Chamber.

Txell organized her first solo runway show in September of 2003. Later that year, she started her own label and joined the Milan-based creative team of designer Neil Barrett. The style of her designs has been compared to the deconstructionist style that marked Japanese fashion in the eighties. Unlike most other designers, she uses the *modélage* technique, in which the designs are tried out directly on the body.

Txell took part in the 2005 Prague Fashion Week, and only one year later was chosen by the Austrian magazine *Unit-F* to participate in a show of young European designers in Vienna. She was a finalist in the 2007 Gen Art Style New York Fashion Awards. Her collections are currently on sale in stores in Spain, the USA, Germany, Belgium, Italy, Greece, Kuwait and Hong Kong.

Sketch from the fall-winter 2006-2007 collection

One garment

"A book-purse I made a few years ago."

Sketches from the fall-winter 2006-2007 collection

Sketch from the fall-winter 2006-2007 collection

Pictures of the fall-winter 2006-2007 collection runway show

Pictures of the fall-winter 2006-2007 collection runway show

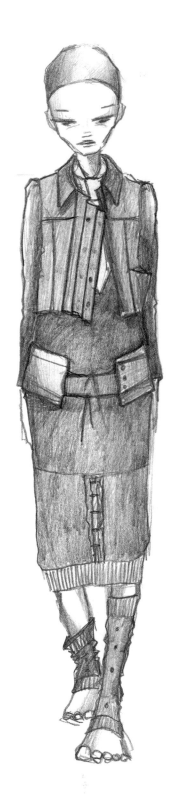

Sketches from the fall-winter 2006-2007 collection

"Not to have
too many
nightmares."

Sketches from the fall-winter 2006-2007 collection

Sketch from the fall-winter 2006-2007 collection

Pictures of the fall-winter 2006-2007 collection runway show

Picturre from the fall-winter 2008-2009 collection runway show

Victorio & Lucchino

www.victorioylucchino.com

One inspiration

"A pink Bignonia in Sanlúcar de Barrameda (Cádiz, Spain)."

The team made up of José Víctor Rodríguez Caro, native of Córdoba, Spain, and José Luis Medina del Corral, a Sevillian, mark a turning point in the history of Spanish fashion over the last twenty years. Since the beginnings of the Victorio & Lucchino label, these two designers of haute couture and prêt-à-porter collections have been recognized around the world for their avant-garde and daring designs inspired by the Sevillian aristocratic circles.

They presented their first collection in 1985 in New York. From the very start, their confident, innovative and somewhat eccentric style was received with great enthusiasm by the fashion media. Their designs highlight the female body and feature typical elements of traditional Andalusian clothing styles such as fringing, ruffles and lace.

The firm currently dresses a long list of celebrities and members of the international jet set. Besides its haute couture and men and women's lines, it also has a highly sought-after line of wedding gowns, worn by many important figures, as well as children's fashion and home lines. Their designs are popular inside and outside Spain, particularly in countries like the USA, Japan, the UK and Italy.

Pictures from the fall-winter 2008-2009 collection runway show

One garment

"An evening gown."

Sketches from the fall-winter 2008-2009 collection and from the fall-winter 2007-2008 collection

Pictures of the fall-winter 2008-2009 collection runway show

Sketch from the spring-summer 2008 bridal collection

Sketches from the spring-summer 2008 collection (left) and from the fall-winter 2007-2008 collection (right)

One dream

"To take our fashion to everybody."

Pictures of the fall-winter 2008-2009 collection runway show

Picture from the fall-winter 2008-2009 collection runway show

Sketch from the fall-winter 2005-2006 collection

Vincenzo
De Cotiis

contatto@studionext.it

One inspiration

"The past. Recycling is an actual and contemporary way to interpret fashion."

Born in Mantua, Italy, Vincenzo De Cotiis graduated in architecture from Milan Polytechnic Universty. His first jobs as an architect, interior designer and fashion designer revealed his skills with malleable materials and his use of restructured elements from the past, and the way he uses and harmonizes color with the environment.

In 1998, he was appointed head of design of the company Haute, a role that involved the development of a prêt-à-porter line of limited edition pieces. Since then and up to now, Vincenzo has enjoyed vintage elements and exquisite fabrics, modernizing them through manual techniques, always as the result of a research and experimentation process. His collections display a truly unique desire for experimentation more than merely trendsetting.

Apart from being a fashion designer that has never opted for the catwalk, Vincenzo is one of the most prestigious interior architects. One of his most recent pieces of work is the Straf Hotel Milan, a proof, once again, that research is always a capital element in his work. The result has been a creative fusion of minimalist design with Italian architectural elements.

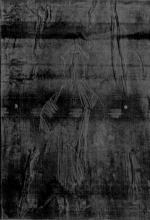

Sketches from the fall-winter 2005-2006 collection

Sketches from the fall-winter 2005-2006 collection

One garment

"Any piece comes out naturally, almost istinctively."

Sketch from the fall-winter 2005-2006 collection

"Dreams are continuous and overbearing."

Sketches from the fall-winter 2005-2006 collection

Sketch from the fall-winter 2005-2006 collection

Vincenzo De Cotiis 445

Picture from the fall-winter 2008-2009 runway show

Yigal Azrouël

www.yigal-azrouel.com

One inspiration

"Music."

Yigal Azrouël, born and bred in Israel, started his career as a fashion designer in 2000 when he opened his creative workshop in the Big Apple, and that very year he presented his first collection during New York Fashion Week. His calling originates from a special creative sensitivity that the designer cultivates with architecture, art, nature and the cultural and daily life of his adoptive city. The success of his first collection led to the opening of his flagship store in the Meatpacking District, one of the New York fashion neighborhoods.

In July 2004, Yigal was named as a member of the prestigious Council of Fashion Designers of America, and was recognized as one of the most visionary creators of North American fashion. Fashion critics praise his self-taught capacity, as well as the special touch he adds to his garments in regards to his use of volume and carefully selected fabrics.

In 2007, he presented his first male collection, to which he soon added other accessories that were all the rage among the city's fashion victims. Fruits of his work are awards such as the Best Current Designer award he received during New York Fashion 2008 and from the famous male fashion magazine *GQ*. That same year, he opened his second store in the area of the Hamptons.

Sketches from the spring-summer 2008 (left) and fall-winter 2008-2009 collections (right)

Sketches from the spring-summer 2008 collection

One garment

"An old leather jacket."

Sketches from the fall-winter 2008-2009 collection

One dream

"Endless…"

Sketch from the fall-winter 2008-2009 collection

Sketch from the fall-winter 2008-2009 collection

Pictures of the fall-winter 2008-2009 collection runway show

Picture of the fall-winter 2008-2009 collection runway show

Picture of the fall-winter 2008-2009 collection runway show

Picture of the fall-winter 2008-2009 collection runway show